The Rise and Fall
of the Sportswoman

American University Studies

Series IX
History

Vol. 180

PETER LANG
New York • Washington, D.C./Baltimore
Bern • Frankfurt am Main • Berlin • Vienna • Paris

Gregory Kent Stanley

The Rise and Fall
of the Sportswoman

Women's Health, Fitness, and Athletics, 1860–1940

PETER LANG
New York • Washington, D.C./Baltimore
Bern • Frankfurt am Main • Berlin • Vienna • Paris

Library of Congress Cataloging-in-Publication Data

Stanley, Gregory Kent.
The rise and fall of the sportswoman: women's health,
fitness, and athletics, 1860–1940/ Gregory Kent Stanley.
p. cm. — (American university studies. Series IX, History; vol. 180)
Includes bibliographical references (p.   ).
1. Sports for women—United States—Public opinion—History. 2. Physical
fitness for women—United States—Public opinion—History. 3. Physical
education for women—United States—Public opinion—History. 4. Women—
Health and hygiene—United States—Public opinion—History. 5. Public
opinion—United States. I. Title. II. Series.
GV709.18.U6S82   796'.0194—dc20   95-30762
ISBN 0-8204-2882-5
ISSN 0740-0462

Die Deutsche Bibliothek-CIP-Einheitsaufnahme

Stanley, Gregory Kent:
The rise and fall of the sportswoman: women's health, fitness, and athletics,
1860–1940/ Gregory Kent Stanley. –New York; Washington, D.C./Baltimore;
Bern; Frankfurt am Main; Berlin; Vienna; Paris: Lang.
(American university studies: Ser. 9, History; Vol. 180)
ISBN 0-8204-2882-5
NE: American university studies/ 09

The paper in this book meets the guidelines for permanence and durability
of the Committee on Production Guidelines for Book Longevity
of the Council of Library Resources.

Printed in the United States of America.

Acknowledgments

At the end of a long task, it is a refreshing diversion to acknowledge those kind souls who have helped along the way. I owe a great deal to Eric Christianson and Mark Summers for helping to clarify earlier drafts. During the early phases of research, I benefited from the advice of Nancy Dye. David Olster, Bob Brigham, and Richard Hamm also gave their advice and encouragement. Thanks also go to Lynn Hiler for her word processing prowess. I cannot even hope to find the words to express my debts to Judy Cornett and Charles E. Stanley. This book is dedicated to my graduate school mentor, Robert D. Cross, a fine gentleman and scholar whose elegant writing style I have long admired.

Table of Contents

Introduction:
In Search of Context

No one questions the prominent role sport plays in society. Yet for decades, academicians shunned sport as a topic, deeming it unscholarly or anti-intellectual. This pattern of neglect could partly be explained by the enormous amount of competition for scholarly attention from other important research topics. Still, this theory does not explain the historical hostility toward the subject. Placing the issue in greater context, it was not just sports history but the entire field of social history that was once held in low regard by many professional historians. Historians tended to possess an elitist educational and social background, and accordingly wrote and taught in an exclusive atmosphere. Some even suggested that an historical analysis of ordinary people was not one that intellectuals were likely to admire.[1]

The 1970s witnessed great progress in the field of social history. As it gained in prestige, sports history also gained a greater following. The earliest sports historians of this period were generally established scholars with publications in traditional topics. For example, in 1975 noted political historian, Marshall Smelser, published his biography of baseball star Babe Ruth. Frequently such writers had to contend with the criticism that they had surrendered their academic integrity in the pursuit of "popular history," or were at least indulging in a frivolous academic divergence.[2]

As sports history attracted more practitioners it also acquired the trappings of legitimacy. A scholarly journal, *The Journal of Sport History*, began publication in 1974. Respected presses and major journals published sports related manuscripts and articles. Sports history has now matured to the point of developing its own historiography. Many writers place sport in the broader context of urban history, with considerable emphasis on the idea of social control as espoused by Robert Wiebe.[3] In addition, the topic has attracted the attention of Marxist historians.[4] Moreover, the portrayal of sport as an intrinsic good has also produced a flood of anti-establishment writings such as Harry Edwards, *The*

Revolt of the Black Athlete, Paul Hoch, *Rip Off the Big Game*, and Gary Shaw, *Meat on the Hoof*.[5]

Conspicuously absent in the literature of sports history are book-length works detailing the history of women's athletics. Donald Mrozek, in his *Sport and American Mentality, 1880-1910*, devotes one chapter to the sportswoman but his chronology sharply limits his focus.[6] Similarly, Martha Verbrugge's *Able-Bodied Womanhood* is limited to the period ending in 1900.[7] A rather rare exception to this trend is Allen Guttmann's recently published *Women's Sports, A History*. The book is very informative, but general in the extreme, covering the period from ancient Egypt to the present.[8] A great many books have taken the form of anthologies of conference papers occasionally mixed with reprinted articles from the late nineteenth and early twentieth centuries.[9] The best example of this approach is *Out of the Bleachers, Writings on Women and Sports* by Stephanie Twin. It contains only the briefest glimmer of her own historical analysis: the rest coming from reprinted primary source articles.[10] Similarly, Ellen Gerber's oft-cited *The American Woman in Sport* is actually the work of four authors although Gerber's contribution (including a very fine bibliography) is the most significant. Her article, "The Controlled Development of Collegiate Sport for Women," in the *Journal of Sport History* is also an excellent but brief work.[11] Furthermore, available works are replete with numerous citations of unpublished conference papers or dissertations. This field is as yet lacking general syntheses and in-depth monographs.

More critically, writings on women's sports have been plagued with a number of perceptual errors. Traditionally, the specific topic of women's sports has been the province of physical education departments. The focus of such works has typically been the exclusion of women from sports and the (sometimes heroic) efforts of individual women to overcome these obstacles. Generally, the key figures that emerge from these works are collegiate physical education instructors of the late nineteenth and early twentieth centuries. To these people go the credit not only for creating women's sports programs but also for eventually destroying them in their quest for total autonomy in the supervision and administration of women's exercise and sport.

Such an interpretation obscures any hint of historical context and fails to take into consideration any development outside of the college. Without denying the importance of collegiate physical education, there exist compelling reasons to question the belief that it was the only important agent of change. In a very basic way, the number of women attending college was far too small for collegiate physical educators to have been solely responsible for determining the nature and limits of women's athletics. Many other social and cultural factors must be considered to explain the rise and fall of women's sports and the cultural symbol of the sportswoman.

Also missing from these accounts is any interaction between the college and American society at large. It is not enough simply to say that many physical education programs for women, and subsequently athletics, did in fact originate in colleges. We must also investigate the social forces which prompted physical educators and college administrators to take such action. Likewise it would be naive to state that collegiate administrators were solely responsible for the decline of women's sports programs and the nearly complete disappearance of any vestige of the sportswoman from the whole fabric of American culture.

To a large extent, such an interpretation is the result of another perceptual error created by a heavy, if not exclusive, reliance on physical education writings as primary sources. This approach is not confined to the ranks of physical education. As Frances Cogan has pointed out in her very fine *All-American Girl, The Ideal of Real Womanhood in Mid-Ninteenth Century America*, many modern works dealing with women's history rely on specialist publications such as suffrage journals or medical texts to tell what "everyone thought" about women's inherent abilities or biological limits. Such analyses are doomed to distortion.[12]

One reason that specialist publications are so heavily used is that many historians distrust popular sources. The current trend has been to dismiss as naive and unsophisticated any straightforward reading of popular writings as primary texts. The result has been a rather curious blindness of what nineteenth century popular writers actually wrote. Some writers, as Cogan notes, substitute in place of primary source information a modernized theoretical model of what such writers should have said.[13]

Such an approach is quite common in the history of women's sports. While it is true that the push for physical exercise did form a vital part of feminist campaigns, not all pro-fitness writers shared the sentiments of women activists. Pro-fitness sources may have praised exercise for women as did such activist authors as Amelia Bloomer or Elizabeth Cady Stanton. But they can in no way be seen as proof of unanimous support for the sportswoman.[14]

Far from echoing any kind of women's rights platform, a great deal of the early literature on the sportswoman is fraught with the rhetoric of inequality. Pro-fitness writers, in numbers far too great to be dismissed, refused to abandon their notions of women's physical limits and proper place in society. They may have favored increased fitness for women but not for the same reasons given by feminist writers.[15] Quite the contrary, their advocacy of exercise addressed the goal of making young women physically fit for their sphere or destiny, in this case motherhood. That is precisely why so many writers lauded exercise for girls and young women, but condemned sports for adult women as unnecessary or even destructive of femininity.

This diversity of support has been overlooked by scholars who have tailored their primary sources too closely. In general, writings on the sportswoman have been complicated by the preconceptions of some historians. As Carroll Smith-Rosenberg pointed out in her thought-provoking *Disorderly Conduct*, much of women's history has been overshadowed by political feminism. Such a close alliance between feminism and women's history has spawned a perceptual problem: namely regarding as important only those sources which confirm the evolution of a feminist consciousness. Consequently, sources which do not fit this line of thought are dismissed as atypical or worse, get wrenched into shape against the evidence. As a result, women's history is too often a study of feminist history alone.[16]

This present study is primarily based on an analysis of health and fitness advice for women derived from a survey of popular press materials, including books and especially such magazines as *Godey's Ladies' Book*, *Living Age*,

Forum, Atlantic Monthly, Cosmopolitan, Collier's, Ladies' Home Journal, and *Good Housekeeping.* By casting the net of historical inquiry more widely, that is by examining a host of popular sources in addition to the professional journals of medical and physical education associations, this work attempts to avoid the distortions of some earlier works. It seeks to place the sportswoman in greater historical context, analyzing the impact of women's sports on American society and vice-versa. In large measure the study seeks to understand how, during the period 1860-1940, the idea of women's exercise and athletics was presented to and accepted by the general public. It explores the factors that influenced the public to accept or to reject the role which women played in athletics. A particular concern is to document and to explain the emergence and decline of the sportswoman as a cultural symbol.

The purpose here is not to write a general history of women's sports or to chronicle women's intercollegiate competition. As worthy of scholarly investigation as those un-worked topics may be, they would require far more time than is currently available to explore the enormous regional diversity that existed in women's colleges.

Chapter one traces the origins of women's sports back to the mid-nineteenth century. At that time the belief was quite common that the health of American men and women had declined over the course of the last generation. In spite of evidence to the contrary, this belief endured throughout the century. Although the health of men and women came under scrutiny, the dominance of medical and popular publications by men often resulted in women being described as much weaker and the true culprit behind many of the nation's perceived problems. Moreover, contemporary thought on heredity, by assigning greater importance to the mother's contribution, intensified the scrutiny of women's health. For if women were weak, the popular theory maintained, they would produce children who were weaker still. The following generations would follow this downward spiral of vitality leading to the destruction of all that was noble and fine in the American character.

One of the debates on women's health in the nineteenth century centered on the issue of education. Chapter two examines the arguments of many medical authorities and social commentators who believed that the intellectual and emotional rigors of collegiate life placed unnatural demands on women, who were thought to have a very limited reservoir of stamina. For these writers, women electing to attend college were, whether willfully or unknowingly, jeopardizing their health. As discussed in chapters three and four, many of the eastern women's colleges were chartered within this rather unpromising environment. The very existence of these schools suggests that some educational promoters believed that women were capable of enduring the demands placed upon them by higher education. College administrators clearly had a vested interest in the health of their students. They had to demonstrate that higher education did not destroy women's health thereby imperiling the nation. As a result, these colleges soon established departments of physical education both to cure existing ill-health and to prevent its occurrence. When the military-style gymnastic drills proved unpopular with students, physical education instructors frequently adopted athletic games.

Many women were indeed introduced to athletics in colleges. Yet had the sportswoman remained an academic phenomenon she would have also remained a minor element of American society. Chapter five details a host of developments at the popular level which introduced the image of the sportswoman to a broader audience. Chief among these developments were the changes in beauty standards during the late nineteenth century. When these changes were complete in the early twentieth century, the slimmer athletic look for women established itself as the dominant standard of beauty.

The appeal of the sportswoman was further enhanced by the growth of expensive and elite country clubs and resorts. These changes meant that the sportswoman would be identified with beauty, sex appeal, leisure, and refined living. A burgeoning post-World War I advertising industry presented this message to the public at-large. Before the twenties had lost its roar, the image of the sportswoman enjoyed what appeared to be a widespread popular endorsement. As a cultural ideal, however, the power of its symbolism could lose force if the narrow range of circumstance in which it flourished were to change.

Chapter six chronicles the eclipse of the sportswoman. During the second half of the 1920s and beyond, several factors contributed to the long-term demise of this widely recognized but never completely accepted symbol. Here we are reminded of John Higham's intonation that social thought and popular sentiment do not change with linear precision. Rather, they ebb and flow. While the popularity of ideas may come and go, the advocacy of their proponents and critics persist. The lands between the high and low tides of opinion are marked by competing, and often ambivalent views.[17]

To sustain the importance of the sportswoman as a cultural symbol required the presence of enough leisure time, money, and popular and professional support for the belief that women's bodies could be made strong enough to endure the rigors of athletic competition. Could women improve their health by exercising? Could health be further improved by athletic competition? Did beauty require a trim body or a full-figure? The varying responses to these questions could reveal public action or discourse contradicting the private confidence. For example, illustrator Charles Dana Gibson did much to popularize the athletic look for women. But when he married socialite Irene Langhorne, she marched down the aisle with her hips heavily padded with material thus conforming to a passing beauty ideal.[18]

In the same way that beauty standards overlapped, contradictory opinions regarding the sportswoman could be found in popular magazines. The same magazine which praised the sportswoman could also carry negative articles. Given the long-standing coexistence of ambivalence, advocacy, and opposition towards exercise and athletic competition, it is not surprising to find that the 1920s, the "Golden Age of Sports," also witnessed strong undercurrents of opposition to competitive athletics, especially for women. By mid-decade, professional physical educators withdrew their support from competitive sports for women. These educators warned that such athletic competition fostered vulgarity and other unfeminine traits, and it must have no place in college life. They also warned that such sports could destroy the mental and physical health of young women. Because there were so few women in college, the sportswoman might have weathered this storm, but not the destructiveness of the economic hurricane that soon followed.

The Great Depression contributed mightily to the downfall of the sportswoman. During the Depression years there was less money for advertising. Advertisers shifted their message from an emphasis on products previously associated with beauty and health to the money-saving virtues of the same group of products. There was also less money for leisure activities, college, or expensive clubs. Moreover, unemployment eroded levels of participation in women's industrial league competition. Most, though not all of the underpinnings of the sportswoman's popularity were removed and her image faded.

All of these factors are acknowledged as important, if not equally so, in the ebb and flow of popular opinion that brought with it the downfall of the sportswoman. Another contributing factor, albeit one not recognized in previous scholarship, needs to be discussed. A broader, more careful reading of primary source material indicates that the idea of the sportswoman never enjoyed strong or unanimous support, even among those writers who advocated increased fitness for women. Many writers praised the healthy and robust sportswoman as a marked improvement over the pale, swooning damsel of the nineteenth century. Yet, these same writers also believed that vigorous or strenuous competitive sports would damage health. When truly competitive industrial leagues and Olympic sports for women became more common, many of these wavering advocates persuaded themselves that the tide of enthusiasm for athletic women had ebbed too far from the shores of common decency and sensible female health. Such diversity of support resulted in considerable disagreement over the limits of female athleticism. The lack of clear advocacy and internal bickering within this last bastion of support propelled the sportswoman into what was to become a thirty year-long period of cultural oblivion.

9

Introduction Notes

1. Roland Dewing, "History of American Sports; Academic Featherbedding or Neglected Area?" *Social Science Journal* (October 1977), p. 78.
2. Marshall Smelser, *The Life that Ruth Built* (New York: Quadrangle, 1975).
3. Robert Wiebe, *The Search for Order, 1877-1920* (New York: Hill and Wang, 1967). For analyses of sports as a facet of urban history, see especially, Stephen Hardy, *How Boston Played: Sport, Recreation, and Community, 1865-1915* (Boston: Northeastern University Press, 1982), and Steven Riess, *City Games: The Evolution of American Urban Society and the Rise of Sports* (Urbana: University of Illinois Press, 1989).
4. For a discussion of Marxist interpretation of sports history, see Allen Guttmann, "Commentary: Who's on First? or, Books on the History of American Sport," *Journal of American History* (September 1979), p. 354.
5. Harry Edwards, *The Revolt of the Black Athlete* (New York: Free Press, 1969); Paul Hoch, *Rip off the Big Game: The Exploitation of Sports by the Power Elite* (New York, 1972); Gary Shaw, *Meat on the Hoof: The Hidden World of Texas Football* (New York: St. Martin's , 1972).
6. Donald Mrozek, *Sport and American Mentality, 1880-1910* (Knoxville: University of Tennessee Press, 1983).
7. Martha Verbrugge, *Able-Bodied Womanhood, Personal Health and Social Change in Nineteenth Century Boston* (New York: Oxford University Press, 1988).
8. Allen Guttmann, *Women's Sports, A History* (New York: Columbia University Press, 1988).
9. See Reet Howell, ed., *Her Story in Sport* (New York: Leisure Press, 1982).
10. Stephanie L. Twin, *Out of the Bleachers, Writings on Women and Sports* (Old Westbury, New York: Feminist Press, 1979).
11. Ellen Gerber, et. al., *The American Woman in Sport* (Reading, Massachusetts: Addison-Wesley, 1974); "The Controlled Development of Collegiate Sport for Women," *Journal of Sport History* (Spring 1975), pp. 1-28.
12. Frances Cogan, *All American Girl. The Ideal of Real Womanhood in Mid-Nineteenth Century America* (Athens: University of Georgia Press, 1989), p. 6.
13. *Ibid.*
14. *Ibid.*, pp. 10, 14.

CHAPTER ONE

A Therapeutic Response: Exercise and the Myth of Declining Health

It has become commonplace to describe the nineteenth century as a period of transition. It was indeed a time of rapid, perhaps bewildering change, characterized among other things by industrialization, immigration, and urbanization. Many observers lamented that society as it had been known, or at least romanticized, seemed to be crumbling under the oppressive weight of change. In general, Americans responded to the challenge with great optimism, believing that growth and development would be an unmitigated good if order could be instilled. To that end a myriad of reform movements sprang up embracing a stunning array of causes.[1]

One notable exception to the optimism of most of these movements was the subject of health. A strong and uncharacteristic pessimism ran through much of the literature of the early and mid-nineteenth century concerning the health of Americans. It was difficult to escape the pervasive but not always correct belief that the health of the nation's citizenry had declined sharply over the course of a generation or two. The nation was thus imperiled and few observers offered much hope of redress. In the midst of the evangelical fervor of other reform movements, the pessimism surrounding the issue of health stood out in bold relief. In a society that presumed inevitable moral and material progress, the nation's apparently deteriorating health seemed puzzling and alarming.[2]

Central to the pessimism which gripped many of the nation's writers stood the belief that the health and vitality of Americans had declined sharply. Reading through the literature of the era, one is struck by the many pronouncements of decline which filled the pages of popular magazines. In general, these writings reflected a gradual but steady abandonment of an earlier, predominantly optimistic view of America's unlimited resources and prospects.[3] In 1862, the *Atlantic Monthly* warned that the evidence "of physical deterioration crowd upon us." The situation was so prevalent that no informed reader could "close the eye to the decaying teeth, distorted form, pallid faces and unseemly gait."[4]

As popularly portrayed, the health, vitality, and resistance of the American people had declined greatly over the last generation. Alex Stevens, president of the New York State Medical Society, recalled that during his early studies abroad it had seemed that Americans were hardier and healthier than Europeans. None of the factors which had such detrimental effects upon the European populations were seen to be operating with anything approaching the same severity in early nineteenth century America. Food was plentiful, unhealthful occupations apparently were few, cities were not yet so large as to endanger health, and epidemics were infrequent.[5] But now he offered a different opinion claiming that America exhibited the same state of ill-health he had seen thirty-five years earlier in Europe.[6]

To prove further that this condition of degeneracy was new, *Godey's Ladies' Book* presented the Revolutionary War generation as a shining example of health and vigor. The magazine urged its readers to think of their grandparents. "They arose at dawn, walked straight on firm legs, had a florid complexion, a ringing laugh."[7] In sharp contrast to this picture of vitality, the current generation appeared liable to fits of weariness. "That neuralgia," the magazine noted, "at which our ancestors would have laughed does too surely dig its talons deep into our brain. Breathlessness seizes us at our every step. We are slender, we are pale." The conclusion was inescapable. This generation, while perhaps being spared the fearful plagues of old, was sickly.[8]

Epidemic diseases, most notably cholera, did much to underscore this sense of decline. Despite attempts to combat them, epidemics continued to appear often exacting a numbing toll, not only in lives, but also in human spirit. In actuality, epidemic diseases seldom took more lives than the deadlier endemic diseases such as tuberculosis. Nevertheless, their spectacular visitations aroused greater fear and anxiety and exposed the shortcomings of standard medical beliefs and practices.

Disagreements within the medical community concerning the very nature of disease only heightened the level of anxiety. Throughout most of the nineteenth century, few Americans (doctors and the lay public alike) believed that diseases such as cholera were contagious. In the era before the germ theory was embraced, disease was not a well-defined biological entity. Medical practitioners, therefore, generally did not believe that diseases were generated by discrete or unique causative agents.[9]

Such uncertainty choked any growth of optimism and also provided an opening whereby other influences could enter the debate. Many observers, for example, saw the wrath of God manifest in the epidemics. Early American diseases could be interpreted then, as divine punishment for sin and sloth. In typical Old Testament style, Philadelphians during the 1793 yellow fever epidemic believed the entire city was being punished for the pride and vanity of its leaders as well as the immorality of the citizenry. After all, they argued, the plague arrived "miraculously" just as the city completed its new Chestnut Street Theater, called by its pious detractors the "Synagogue of Satan."[10]

The link between disease and morality was strong and persistent. It was widely considered that disease only struck the intemperate or the unchristian. Thus, most Americans were little surprised when the "lower order" succumbed so readily and in such great numbers. In 1832, the governor of New York stated that the cholera epidemic had come about because "an infinitely wise and just God has seen fit to employ pestilence as one means of scourging the human race for its sins..."[11] Cholera was a disease with profound social and moral implications. To contract the disease was socially inexcusable. To die from it was indeed very suspicious. It was God's judgment for sin. Accordingly, the "respectable persons of regular habits" reassured themselves that they had little to fear.[12]

Proclamations that disease struck only the poor or the sinful were not entirely comforting. In the long run, unseen bacteria proved to be no respecters of social position, infecting the high and low with a great deal of republican egalitarianism. Many Americans thus looked for other, more palatable explanations. Doctors advocated a number of environmental theories. For example, Dr. Edward H. Barton, the leading physician of New Orleans in the early nineteenth century, was quite adamant that changes in weather brought about disease. He claimed that "various proportions of heat and moisture" could explain almost everything in relation to health. He kept meticulous meteorological records which he believed indicated a clear link between weather and disease. According to his statistics, local yellow fever epidemics occurred only during periods of elevated temperature combined with undue moisture.[13] So popular was the idea that in 1818, the Surgeon-General ordered that surgeons of every regiment keep a diary of the weather noting everything of importance relating to medical topography. Quarterly reports based upon those findings were to be sent to Washington, D.C. for analysis. [14]

Another popular environmentally linked theory of disease origins focused on what was loosely termed the "atmosphere." Disease, according to this theory was a pestilence caused by poisons in the air. As the *Nation* explained, these poisons were most often released by decaying organic matter. Once air-borne, these miasmas clung to clothing, houses, and soil, and people unconsciously ingested them by eating, drinking, or breathing.[15] Health authorities, therefore, devoted their attention to those items in the environment which they thought might cause disease such as manure piles, cesspools, decaying leaves, rubbish and dead animals.[16] One doctor, for example, warned a friend to move some rotten potatoes from his barn lest his stablehand who lived there should contract cholera.[17]

The great weakness of this theory lay in its inability to explain why some people in a specific place were stricken while other were not.[18] If miasmas were, as the *Nation* theorized, localized and "altogether inert," something had to trigger the actual outbreak of disease. Some "exciting cause" was required to activate the latent poisons.[19] The most popular explanation given by medical popularizers for this causative agent centered on the idea of predisposition. As Dr. Jonathan Wilson explained to the readers of *Godey's Ladies' Book,* diseases such as diphtheria or cholera were in fact "diseases of debility." As such, no one was ever attacked unless they had somehow weakened or predisposed themselves by "habits of life, eating, drinking, air, or other surroundings".[20] Health (or lack thereof) resulted from the interaction between a person's constitutional endowment and the environment.

This belief in predisposition helped to shore up the atmospheric theory of disease. After all, no two constitutions were alike. According to one Massachusetts physician, thousands of variables made up a patient's constitution, including locality, station, occupation, diet, and countless other factors which had acted upon the individual since birth.[21] Those people with a large amount of what *Living Age* termed constitutional vitality would be able to resist the invasion of disease. Conversely, those whose constitutions had been weakened would be the first attacked by the poisons in the air, and the first to die during any epidemic.[22]

Such a connection between constitutional vitality and health fitted neatly into the moral context because a system could be attacked not only by heat, cold, or contaminated air, but also by improper or immoral habits.[23] The theory of predisposition united scientific theories with the much older belief in sin as a cause of disease. Sickness could still be seen as the result of a personal failing because only those individuals who had weakened themselves fell victim to the latent poisons in the air.[24]

Guided by theories scarcely changed since the days of Galen, physicians did not believe that specific agents generated specific diseases. Instead, they pointed to a variety of destablizing factors acting to unbalance a particular constitution. If there were indeed only one cause of disease (systemic unbalance cause by localized inflammation), then only a few treatments would be needed to treat the symptoms of any illness. The object of these "heroic" treatments would of course be to restore natural balance; usually by depleting the patient.

Physicians accomplished this task by bleeding their patients or by purging them through the use of strong emetics such as tartar emetic. In addition, strong cathartic drugs such as the mercury compound calomel enjoyed widespread use. By his ability to "regulate the secretions," to balance intake and outgo, the doctor could offer hope that balance was being restored. The very severity of the drugs used further assured the patients and their families that decisive and forceful action was indeed being taken. Calomel especially produced fast and very noticeable effects including diarrhea, involuntary salivation, profuse sweating, and necrosis of the gums. These symptoms (actually the signatures of mercury poisoning) were seen as proof that the drug was exerting an "alterative effect." Although other drugs produced similar results, mercury was chosen most frequently because it produced swifter results, even in moderate doses.[25]

Heroic treatments, especially those using heavy metal drugs such as calomel or arsenic were at best ineffective and frequently dangerous. It is not surprising, therefore, that patients subjected to them often lost confidence in regular medicine. The cholera epidemics especially did much to focus attention on the disputes within the medical profession and certainly on the unsuccessful modes of treatment. Physicians bled, purged, and administered massive doses of calomel, but the disease still exacted a frightful toll. These unsuccessful methods shook the already insecure public confidence in regular medicine and patients began to seek relief elsewhere. Noting this discontent, unorthodox physicians and various medical sectarians stepped up their attacks on dangerous and excessive drugging. Challenging the regular profession's hegemony by criticizing its therapeutics, and especially by competing with it for patients, the various sectarians did much to erode further the status of established medicine.[26]

Critics of heroic medicine heralded the healing power of nature and the tendency of disease to run its course if left alone. Yet, even these critics, it should be remembered, were not truly inactive in actual practice. In the sickroom they did not hesitate to employ the leading therapies such as bleeding, leeching, mercurial purgatives, or opium. Their practices were, however, much milder than heroic medicine. In addition, they also added to their program careful attention to such "natural" therapies as diet, rest, and exercise.[27]

As a result of these debates and struggles, a new concept of health slowly emerged in the decades after mid-century. Sickness and its treatment were no longer the sole end of medicine. Negative health, as the *Atlantic Monthly* explained, "the mere keeping out of the hospital for a series of years" was not health. The goal should not be simply to get well, but to keep well."[28] Debility by definition, therefore, became not so much the presence of disease, as the absence of full vitality.

The reign of heroic medicine had convinced many health advocates that treatment alone was ineffective and sometimes dangerous. Accordingly, prevention was more greatly desired than treatment. If by adherence to nature's laws of exercise, diet, and hygiene one could preserve the full endowment of vitality, then resistance to all diseases would follow. Increasingly, popular and medical writers praised the saving virtues of physical exercise. In 1867, *Godey's* declared that exercise was "positively necessary for the preservation of our health and physical development."[29] Exercise was thus elevated to the lofty level of what the *Atlantic Monthly* termed the "great law of the universe." When the life forces ran low, exercise was the "natural and most effectual method of invigorating those forces." [30] With health, one threw off the assaults of disease that leveled others. Writing for *Popular Science Monthly*, Dr. F.L. Oswald was bold enough to proclaim that ninety percent of all diseases could in fact be cured by exercise. It accelerated blood circulation and stimulated the internal organs, thereby counteracting innumerable disorders. A body able to perform athletic feats would be protected from "any morbid element." Such advice, he concluded, had great implications for patients wary of heroic treatments. Sickness could now be cured mechanically, by exercise ("by climbing a tree, or chopping it down, if you prefer") instead of chemically, by swallowing drugs.[31]

Famed education reformer Horace Mann also lent his polished prose in support of exercise. In 1855, he lauded gymnastics for safeguarding the body against sickness. Horrid diseases, such as bronchitis and asthma were thus exorcised and driven from the body. Dyspepsia lost its hold, he stated, when its victim mounted the gymnastic horse and untold "legion of blue devils were impaled" upon the parallel bars.[32]

These writers were very specific as to which exact type of exercise was most beneficial. Answering its own rhetorical question of how vigor was reached, the *Atlantic Monthly* announced in 1862 that "speaking in a general way, those exercises in which the lungs and heart are made to go at a vigorous pace are to be ranked among the most useful."[33] Similarly, *Godey's* announced that if a person's lungs were not well developed, then health would be imperfect. The magazine held out one hopeful prospect by noting that chest size, and consequently lung capacity, could be increased dramatically in a few months by careful exercise. Specifically, *Godey's* advocated "daily out-door running with the mouth closed, beginning with twenty yards and back at a time, increasing ten yards every week until a hundred are gone over thrice a day."[34]

Health reformers and exercise advocates focused a great deal of attention on the subject of lung capacity. At that time, the prevalence of lung diseases, especially tuberculosis, was a constant and frightening fact of life. Conflicting medical opinions on the workings of such diseases only added to these fears. Potential causes for lung disorders, therefore, were many. Dio Lewis, leading advocate of physical training in the mid- and late-nineteenth century, firmly believed that the major cause of tuberculosis was a contracted chest, which lessened the "space for the play of those organs contained within it." If the chest were expanded, "respiration would be perfected and resistance increased."[35]

Out-door exercise became mandatory elements of physical training programs. Lung conditioning was of little use, however, unless performed in fresh air. Respired air was considered dangerous because, many thought, it was rendered impure by the mere act of breathing.[36] This was an unsettling situation, because a person could be weakened by foul air and not be aware of it. Advocates of exercise, therefore, also heralded the importance of ventilation. Lewis urged people to sleep with their windows open, for "if the air of the bed chamber be impure, the complexion, eyes, and nerves must soon suffer."[37] Even ordinarily healthful exercise, if performed in the impure air of rooms "warmed and vitiated by many contaminating breaths," could impair if not utterly destroy the strongest constitution.[38] *Godey's* explained that as winter approached, many people refrained from venturing out-doors for fear of catching cold. This was a very unwise course of action because those who passed months without breathing fresh air became so enfeebled that their constitutions had no power to resist. They soon fell victim, not simply to colds, but to worse diseases such a tuberculosis.[39]

The prescription of exercise found great favor with a very vocal group of writers who blamed American ill-health on the rise of the city. Urbanization had long stood at the center of much that was new and troubling. Crowded cities in which piles of garbage festered, privies overflowed, and dead animals lay where they fell did indeed create intolerable conditions.[40] They served as hosts for diseases such as typhus, diphtheria, and the most deadly scourge, tuberculosis.

In addition, many onlookers blamed the city for producing a new form of disease. According to the *Atlantic Monthly*, the peril of the city was in living too fast. The resultant excitement of this rapid pace was debilitating.[41] As early as 1860, the editors of *Godey's* had linked insanity to the excitement of life inherent in modern urban America.[42] Many other periodicals suggested that the city's most grievous danger was the disproportionate increase in diseases of the mind. The strain involved in adjusting to the new, complex, and rapidly changing order fell most heavily upon the urban professional and mercantile classes.[43] In the cities, the new order demanded a preponderance of labor of the brain over that of the muscles. In every direction, the modern urban dweller was more heavily taxed as "brain work" multiplied. The result was a new disease of urban America labelled nervousness.

According to Dr. George Beard, chief popularizer of the concept, modern nervousness or "neurasthenia" was "the cry of the system struggling with its environment."[44] It accompanied modern civilization and as such was a nineteenth century American development found more so in cities and at the desk. People in their original state (before modern civilization) could withstand much more stress because the amount of reserve nerve force was so great.[45] But the mental excitement produced by modern living became debilitating when taken in excess. As a result, the "vitality and nervous energy of our people" was being overdrawn at a "rapid and ruinous rate."[46] Physicians considered nervous energy limited and believed that contemporary society placed inordinate demands on that fixed supply.

The common analogy used to describe this situation was that of an overdrawn bank account.[47] Some people were very poor in nerve force, "and if from over-toil, or sorrow, or injury, they overdraw their little surplus, they may find that it will require months, or perhaps years to make up the deficiency...."[48] Nervous exhaustion had profound physical implications. Anything which weakened or wore out the body's nervous energy also weakened the body and exposed it to the numerous diseases of debility.[49] If the body could not withstand the mental strains of life, the result would be an unsound constitution and an ill-developed, sickly body.[50] Not only had the city subjected people to draining new brain work, but it also conspired against health by introducing sedentary lifestyles. The city weakened their minds by drawing off nervous reserves, and weakened their bodies by sparing the urban professional classes the "rigors of the frontier." As a result, they were falling victim to disease such as dyspepsia, neurasthenia, and tuberculosis.[51] In 1861, the *Atlantic Monthly* complained that as all handwork was transmuted into brain-work, people became sedentary. The body thus suffered and needed something to restore vitality.[52]

This new form of disease required a new therapeutic approach. Nervous exhaustion produced disease by draining off vital energy. Consequently, it would only be worsened by depletive therapies, such as bleeding or purging. Such a condition called instead for stimulative therapy. After mid-century, stimulants such as whiskey, quinine, and cinchona bark became the treatments of choice for many physicians.[53]

Exercise fit neatly into the more natural program of stimulative therapy. It strengthened the body and built up nervous reserves and was thus a near perfect prescription for people debilitated by the new strains of urban living. It enabled a person to resist the harmful tendencies of city life. Writing for *Godey's Ladies' Book*, Dr. Jonathan Wilson warned his readers that the intensive mental application so characteristic of urban professional work diminished vitality. Consequently, writers, literary people, or anyone compelled to sit at a desk for long periods must devote regular intervals to exercise. The exercise "should be as prolonged and as vigorous as bodily strength will allow." Wilson recommended running up flights of stairs."[54]

To prove that advanced civilization did not necessarily entail the loss of strength and vitality, many writers pointed to the ancient Greeks. Not only were they superior scholars, artists, and philosophers, a *North American Review* author stated, but they were also fountains of great vital force because they "gymnasticized themselves into power."[55] The author further noted that Herodicus, celebrated teacher of Hippocrates, cured himself of disease through gymnastics and lived to the age of one hundred. He also told his readers that

Galen, the great medical philosopher, had been feeble until he was thirty years old but became strong and healthy by devoting several hours each day to gymnastic exercise.[56]

The crusades for fresh air and exercise were firmly rooted in the health reform movements of the nineteenth century. They were active therapeutic responses to the threat (real or imagined) of debility and its dire consequences. The prescription of exercise blended very well with the doctrine of personal responsibility and further strengthened the idea that men and women had to take the initiative to preserve their own health. In some ways this belief enabled people to assume some measure of control in the face of baffling sicknesses, as failure to maintain health was in essence a personal failing.[57] If the nation were to survive the new challenges placed before it, its citizens must also take responsibility for their health as well. Exercise thus became a widely-prescribed non-heroic means of building the strength and vigor needed to combat the perils of the new urban age.

Chapter One Notes

1. See among others, Ronald G. Walters, *American Reformers, 1815-1860* (New York: Hill and Wang, 1978).
2. Charles Rosenberg, *The Care of Strangers, The Rise of the Hospital System* (New York: Basic Books, 1987).
3. James Cassedy, *Medicine and American Growth, 1800-1869* (Madison: University of Wisconsin Press, 1986), p. 208.
4. "The New Gymnastics," *Atlantic Monthly* (August 1862), p. 129.
5. Charles Rosenberg, *The Cholera Years* (Chicago: University of Chicago Press, 1962), p. 144. Stevens' remark is dated 1844.
6. *Ibid.*, p. 13.
7. *Ibid.*
8. "Editors' Table: Weariness of the World and its Work," *Godey's Ladies' Book* (August 1864), p. 173.
9. John Harley Warner, *The Therapeutic Perspective. Medical Practice, Knowledge and Identity in America, 1820-1865* (Cambridge: Harvard University Press, 1986), p. 86.
10. Martin S. Pernick, "Politics, Parties, and Pestilence: Epidemic Yellow Fever in Philadelphia and the Rise of the First Party System," in Judith Walzer Leavitt and Ronald L. Numbers, eds., *Sickness and Health in America* 2d. ed., (Madison: University of Wisconsin Press, 1985), pp. 360-361.
11. Rosenberg, *The Cholera Years*, p. 41. For more recent works see Pernick, "Parties, Politics and Pestilence," and John Blake, "The Inoculation Controversy in Boston, 1721-1722," in Leavitt and Numbers, *Sickness and Health in America*.
12. Rosenberg, *The Cholera Years*, p. 29.
13. Cassedy, *Medicine and American Growth*, pp. 42-43.
14. *Ibid.*, pp. 44-45.
15. "Sanitary Drainage," *Nation* (July 6, 1876), p. 13; "A Few Words About Cholera," *Nation* (September 7, 1865), p. 308; "Facts and Opinions About the Cholera," *Nation* (April 26, 1866), p. 520.
16. Francis Robbins Allen, "Public Health in the Southeast, 1872-1941: The Study of a Social Movement," (Ph.d. dissertation, University of North Carolina, 1946), p. 78, see also, J.S. Chambers, M.D., *The Conquest of Cholera. America's Greatest Scourge* (New York: Macmillan, 1938), p. 35.
17. Chambers, *The Conquest of Cholera*, p. 139.
18. Rosenberg, *The Cholera Years*, p. 76.

19. "A Few Words About Cholera," *Nation* (September 7, 1865), p. 308.

20. Dr. Jonathan Wilson, "Hints About Health," *Godey's Ladies' Book* (October 1865), p. 360. See also, Wilson, "Health Department," *Godey's Ladies' Book* (November 1863), pp. 481-482; and Wilson, "Hints About Health," *Godey's Ladies' Book* (August 1866), p. 173.

21. Warner, *Therapeutic Perspective*, p. 64.

22. "Vitality Versus Disease," *Living Age* (April 15, 1862), p. 26; see also Elisha Harris, "Cholera Prevention," *Nation* (October 3, 1867), p. 273.

23. Warner, *Therapeutic Perspective*, p. 86.

24. Rosenberg, *The Cholera Years*, pp.76-77.

25. *Ibid.*, pp. 41-42.

26. Warner, *Therapeutic Perspective*, p. 52.

27. *Ibid., p. 129.*

28. "Gymnastics," *Atlantic Monthly* (March 1861), p. 301.

29. "Hints About Health," *Godey's Ladies' Book* (September 1867), p. 265.

30. "Weak Lungs and How to Make Them Strong," *Atlantic Monthly* (June 1873), p. 668.

31. "F.L. Oswald, M.D., "The Age of Gymnastics," *Popular Science* (June 1873), p. 668.

32. Cited in "Gymnastics," *North American Review* (July 31, 1855), p. 62.

33. "New Gymnastics," *North American Review* (July 1855), p. 62.

34. "Hints About Health," *Godey's Ladies' Book* (September 1866), pp. 263-264.

35. Dio Lewis, *The New Gymnastics for Men, Women, and Children* (Boston: Tichenor and Fields, 1862), pp. 265-268.

36. Harvey Green, *Fit for America. Health, Fitness, Sport, and American Society* (New York: Pantheon, 1986), p. 78.

37. Dio Lewis, *Our Girls* (New York: Harper and Brothers, 1871), p. 344.

38. "Hints About Health," *Godey's Ladies' Book* (September 1867), p. 265.

39. "Death In-Doors," *Godey's Ladies' Book* (November 1867), p. 449.

40. Leavitt and Numbers, eds., *Sickness and Health in America*, pp. 3-4.

41. "Gymnastics," *Atlantic Monthly* (March 1861), p. 297.

42. Cited in Harvey Green, *The Light of the Home. An Intimate View of the Lives of Women in Victorian America* (New York: Pantheon, 1983), p. 136.

43. William DeWitt Hyde, "A Rational System of Physical Training," *Forum* (June 1891), p. 451.

44. George Beard, *American Nervousness, Its Causes and Consequences* (New York: Putnam's Sons, 1881), reprint ed., Arno Press, 1972, pp. 26, 137-138.

24

45. Ibid., pp. 5, 26, 138, 183. For a more recent work, see Janet Oppenheim, *Shattered Nerves. Doctors, Patients, and Depression in Victorian England* (New York: Oxford University Press, 1991).

46. "Gymnastics," *Atlantic Monthly* (March 1861), p. 297; Hyde, "A Rational System of Physical Training," *Forum* (June 1991), p. 451, see also, Rosenberg, *The Care of Strangers*.

47. For a fuller description see especially, James Whorton, *Crusaders for Fitness. The History of American Health Reform* (Princeton University Press, 1982).

48. Beard, *American Nervousness*, pp. 9-10.

49. Dr. Charles P. Uhle, "Health Department," *Godey's Ladies' Book* (February 1871), p. 191.

50. G. Mercer Adam, ed., *Sandow on Physical Training, A Study in Perfect Form* (New York: J. Selwin Tait and Sons, 1894), p. 4.

51. Green, *Fit for America*, p. 320.

52. "Gymnastics," *Atlantic Monthly* (March 1861), p. 285.

53. Warner, *The Therapeutic Perspective*, p. 98.

54. Dr. Jonathan Stainback Wilson, "Health Department," *Godey's Ladies' Book* (January 1860), p. 82.

55. "Gymnastics," *North American Review* (July 1855), pp. 53, 59.

56. *Ibid.*, p. 59.

57. Oppenheim, *Shattered Nerves*, p. 92.

CHAPTER TWO

A Harsh Indictment: Portrayals of Women's Health in Nineteenth-Century American Thought

Although decrying the health of all Americans, medical and popular writers alike reserved their strongest criticism for the state of women's health. *Godey's Ladies' Book*, for example, claimed that American women as a general class were fragile, delicate, and incapable of enduring any hardship. As a result, many had become helpless invalids, "to say nothing of those resting in their graves."[1] Writers from various sectors repeated this harsh indictment so often that it became a pervasive feature of medical and popular literature.

As did many writers, Dr. George Beard wrote that this condition was a recent and distinctly American phenomenon. He could think of no other age, country, or civilization in the days of their glory which were beset with such maladies. In America, he noted, feebleness had so become the norm that "the first observation of a European that lands upon our shore is that our women are a feeble race."[2] Similarly, Catherine Beecher labelled the increase of disease among mature women and young girls as most alarming. She too believed that the prevalence of sickness was "never known in any former period."[3]

With great regularity, doctors, scholars, and a host of popular writers dealt with the much advertised problem of declining health by blaming American women. Not only were women apparently weaker than men, but this weakness seemed to pose a greater threat. In 1863, *Godey's* medical editor, Dr. Jonathan Stainback Wilson, asserted that any hope of reform hinged upon women. He proclaimed that women "must be the principal agent in health reform. They must correct their own bad habits of living before the streams of health can flow out for the healing of the nation."[4] In nearly identical language, Dr. Samuel Gregory wrote for *Living Age* that women, by preserving their own health, would also secure the "constitutional well-being of the rising race."[5]

When physicians wrote about the poor health of women, they were often thinking about the children such women might produce. According to nineteenth century medical thinking, nervous mothers bore nervous children.[6] As Catherine Beecher wrote, the present generation of parents gave their children, "so far as the mother has hereditary influence, feebler constitutions than the former generation received." As a result, young children started life with "a more delicate organization than the previous generation."[7]

Predictably, the reproductive capacity of women made them the prime target for health reform. Although both parents influenced heredity, women seemed likely to exert a more profound effect. *Popular Science* in 1874, for instance, declared that mothers must shoulder the burden of improving the health of the American people. As editor Edward Youmans explained, a woman's role in producing healthy children was "more immediate and vital than man's."[8] Even a fetus with excellent traits from the father could be damaged by the chronic weakness of the mother. *Godey's* was also quite explicit that whereas "the offspring partakes of the nature of both parents, the mother possesses the greater modifying power, because the life of the child is bound up with hers prior to its birth, the blood of the two being commingled up to this time."[9]

The *Atlantic Monthly* made an even bolder statement stressing the paramount influence of mothers. In 1862, the author of "The Health of Our Girls" warned that "unless they [mothers] are healthy, the country is not safe." The writer further stated that the importance of healthy mothers was magnified in a democracy because "the fate of our institutions may hang on the precise temperament which our next president shall have inherited from his mother." No mention was made of the hypothetical father.[10]

Women, to a greater degree, controlled the health and vitality of the next generation. Yet the perceived weakness of women combined with the beliefs in the inheritance of acquired traits made many observers despair for the future. These beliefs were firmly implanted in popular thinking. *Godey's* Dr. Jonathan Wilson declared assertively that "the transmission of intellectual, moral, and bodily peculiarities from parents to children is one of the most important and best established facts in physiology." Moreover, he continued, this transmitting or modifying power embraced not only "the original qualities" of the parents, but extended also "to those that are acquired by indulgence in bad habits."[11] Parents (especially mothers) weakened by nervous exhaustion or by bad habits such as tobacco, coffee, tea, alcohol, or improper dress, would then corrupt the health of the unborn. An actual disease Wilson reminded his readers, was not always transmitted directly from mother to child. Instead, in most cases, there would be "a hidden weakness, a constitutional proneness to disease" that would "invite its invasion, and cause the unfortunate child to sink under attacks through which it might have safely passed or entirely escaped."[12]

Such rampant ill-health could be more than a temporary condition. For if women conceived children during a period of weakness, they passed on destruction to the future.[13] Through this process, weakness and nervous debility developed rapidly and became an element in a family's history. By the "remorseless law of inheritance" mothers, therefore, gave birth to weak children who in turn conferred upon their offspring a lower and lower vitality.[14] This downward spiral of degeneracy would continue until national strength collapsed under the burden of inherited weakness.[15]

Even after birth, a child could still be endangered by the mother's level of health. According to popular belief, nursing mothers exerted profound influence over the newborn. The infant was nourished by the milk of the mother which was itself "much influenced as to its quantity and quality by her [mother's] mental and bodily condition."[16] It was a well-established fact, *Godey's* proclaimed, "that anger, grief, fretfulness, envy, and all the depressing passions" of the mother controlled the supply of milk. If a mother were overwrought or exhausted, her milk could easily convert "from the most mild and wholesome of nutriments" to an "irritative poison, capable of producing convulsions, colic, and a train of the most serious disorders."[17] Dr. Beard complained that in America, thousands of mothers could not nurse for they could not bear the fatigue and drain upon the nervous system. He noted that among the upper classes especially, the entire process of gestation and child bearing proceeded in a most unsatisfactory way. Very often these women, weakened by nervous exhaustion, suffered permanent injury or illness brought on by giving birth.[18]

Many American women, unable to nurse their own children had, it seemed, resorted to hiring nurses. At that time few alternatives to breast milk existed and uncontaminated cow's milk was not always plentiful. Also, many mothers chose a wet nurse over one of the new (and supposedly scientific) commercial formulae because human milk appeared to have certain health-promoting qualities that no artificial concoction could provide. Yet for some writers, the very prevalence of this practice was in itself a clear sign of disease, degeneracy, and weakness.[19] Dr. Edward H. Dixon went further stating that a mother's failure to nurse her own baby was an unnatural sin and would lead to many diseases (for the mother), including cancer, tuberculosis, and stroke.[20]

In a sharply worded article, *Godey's* pointedly reminded its readers that the nursing woman (mother or hired nurse) transmitted her physical, mental, and moral condition to the child. If a woman were driven by necessity to hire a nurse, great caution must be exerted. A physician must examine the physical condition of the prospective nurse. To further safeguard the well-being of the infant, the parents of the child must carefully scrutinize the nurse's background. The moral fiber of nurses was often a pressing concern, for many came from the ranks of unwed mothers who had recently given birth and needed temporary shelter.[21] *Godey's* reserved its most vitriolic prose for the practice of hiring foreigners as nurses. The very idea of committing an American child to "any Irish woman or freshly imported foreigner," was utterly unthinkable."[22]

To solve this problem, the city of Boston attempted to compile a wet nurse directory to refer reliable and acceptable nurses to private families. In some areas, arrangements could be made to have recently collected milk delivered but such programs were often frowned upon. By far, a live-in nurse was greatly preferred because a family could carefully monitor her actions thereby lessening the concern over the heritability of moral character through the nurse's milk.[23]

The critical question, then, centered on what had caused this weakness of American women. To that end, a great many physicians, scholars, and writers turned their attention to this threatening predicament. With unfailing regularity, they focused on the female reproductive system, believing it to be the root cause of debility. Historians have frequently pointed out the obsessive manner in which nineteenth century doctors directed their attention to the womb as the sole source of sickness in women, ignoring a host of other possible explanations. Because hormones and the endocrine system remained mysteries until the twentieth century, most physicians were often baffled by the ills of their women patients. As a result, many medical experts traced female illness to the reproductive organs in general and to menstruation in particular, which they depicted as a distinct sickness in itself.[24]

This diagnosis was further reinforced by the persistent belief that the uterus was connected to the central nervous system. Accordingly, any shocks to the reproductive organs would damage the nervous system and vice-versa. Women, it seemed were controlled by their reproductive system. As one doctor wrote, a woman's sexual organs were "preeiminent," and exercised "a controlling influence upon her entire system."[25] So dominant were these organs that another physician, addressing a medical society in 1870, stated that it was almost "as if the Almighty in creating the female sex had taken the uterus and built up a woman around it."[26]

In general, the medical community described the uterus as a perilous possession. Dr. William DeWees, professor of medicine at the University of Pennsylvania, believed that women were subjected to twice the amount of sickness as men, simply because they had a womb.[27] The resultant message could be quite daunting. If medical rhetoric were indeed correct, then all phases of a woman's reproductive life could be a source of sickness. Using a trite metaphor, Dr. George Engleman, president of the American Gynecology Society, stated that even if a young woman were not battered on the breakers of puberty, she could still be dashed to pieces on the rocks of childbirth, ground upon the recurring shallows of menstruation, or marooned on the final bar of menopause, before protection was found "in the unruffled waters of the harbor beyond reach of sexual storms."[28]

One of the most eloquent and influential voices in this particular argument belonged to Dr. Edward Clarke of the Harvard Medical School. His immensely popular *Sex in Education; or a Fair Chance for the Girls* became the central work, either to be applauded or attacked. In this work, Clarke very specifically singled out one abuse of the nervous system as the major cause of weakness among women. "To a large extent," he diagnosed, "our present system of educating girls is the cause of this pallor and weakness."[29] He believed that for far too long, education (by stimulating the brain) had made unhealthful demands upon the internal organs of women, especially the reproductive organs. He then proceeded to analyze both the physical and psychological effects of education.

Central to Clarke's argument stood the belief that educating girls after the onset of puberty was a fundamental mistake. Nature, he claimed, had reserved this time for the process of ovulation and for the development and perfection of the reproductive system. Education interfered with this critical process because the body never did two things well at the same time. Both the muscles and the brain could not work in their best way simultaneously because when the body spent energy in one direction, it then economized in another. If the schoolmaster, therefore, overworked the brains of his pupils, he diverted vital force that would (especially for girls) be needed elsewhere.[30]

In popular thinking, each person possessed a fixed amount of vital energy. Moreover, since the female reproductive system required more vital force than that of men, women had less energy for physical or mental development. Consequently, they could ill-afford any drain upon that supply. For physicians, these statements were so obvious and so ingrained in popular thought, that they required no real proof.[31]

The double-standard here is clear. For boys, puberty marked the onset of strength and vigor. Some writers even suggested that boys should engage in strenuous physical activities to burn off their excess energy.[32] Women, however, had no such surplus. For them, puberty (as commonly thought) marked the beginning of prolonged and periodic weaknesses which at the very least sapped their strength and energy. All available energy, therefore, was needed to meet the stress of these repeated crises. Both muscular and brain labor must be remitted to yield sufficient force for this work.[33]

For some observers, nature exacted a terrible price for the mistakes of youth. If a girl at the onset of puberty violated "the laws of her body," pain, disease, and sterility would follow.[34] It was a fact not to be ignored, the *Atlantic Monthly* reported, that some of the strongest girls had lost their health and had become invalids, simply by being allowed to live the careless or indiscreet life on which boys flourished.[35] Clarke especially warned parents and educators that they must learn that girls could not be trained as boys and still retain uninjured health and a future secure from neuralgia, uterine disease, or hysteria.[36]

Such dire warnings were often taken to heart by the parents of young women. One Victorian-era woman, for example, recalled in her autobiography wanting very much to attend Bryn Mawr. Her parents, however, strongly objected fearing that college life would endanger her health. They pointed to the girl's cousin who had died at the age of twenty-one after leaving Bryn Mawr. Although her death was caused by typhoid and occurred a whole year after leaving school, many family members attributed the death to overwork at college.[37]

Opponents of education thus argued fiercely that the mental strain of study would sap women's physical resources. Grave and even fatal diseases were not uncommon results, as the sick chamber and the hospital confirmed. Clarke lamented that the number of strong, hardy, and cheerful girls from "the bright New England kitchens of old" declined daily. In their place now came the fragile, easily fatigued, languid girls of the modern age. They graduated from school (or worse, college) excellent scholars and well-drilled in books. Yet as a tragic consequence of education, their ovaries remained underdeveloped and many had become completely sterile.[38]

Thoughts of women rendered sterile by education certainly created more than a little concern. Yet Clarke's description of the psychological impact of education caused an even greater commotion. He believed that educating women produced not only physical damage but also a profound character change as well. Central to this change was a general coarsening of all things feminine and especially the disappearance of maternal instincts. Clarke thus painted the image of middle-class American women who either could not bear children, or even more sinister, had no desire to do so.[39]

Education clearly stood as Clarke's prime target, yet for many other writers it was only part of a much larger problem. For these experts, education was merely one of the symptoms of a general change in the behavior of women which seemed antithetical to the future good of the race. The *Forum* was especially vocal on this point, claiming that education posed a threat because it made young women ambitious "to be somebody." Consequently, in an effort to secure or maintain social position, they scorned marriage and especially motherhood. The modern woman who was content with marriage, maternity, and domestic life was "as rare a being as the black swan of the past." Instead, women now busied themselves seeking such distractions as art, politics, or money-making.[40] The magazine labelled this deliberate avoidance of child-bearing as the most evil tendency at work in the nation.[41]

Ambition for luxury, social position, and education worked to "unsex" the middle-class woman. One study claimed that only twenty-eight percent of women college graduates married, compared to eighty percent of women in general.[42] It seemed that educated women had become too highly developed to submit to child-bearing, motherhood, or even marriage. Health advocate Dio Lewis confessed with alarm that among Yankee women, marriage and children had become unfashionable.[43]

Some writers tried to change the tone of the discussion slightly by insisting that they supported women's higher education in principle but that colleges failed by not offering courses designed for the severe constitutional limits of women. In addition, as Edward Youmans stated in an 1874 *Popular Science* editorial, existing women's colleges were liable to criticism for being mere imitations of male establishments. As such, they did not prepare women for maternity, child care, or domestic life. If education were to aid rather than obstruct "the true course of feminine cultivation," newer, more feminine educational institutions must be created to meet the life needs of the female student.[44] Similarly, another *Popular Science* author lamented that what was in vogue at women's colleges was a scheme for the production of literary women who would ultimately sacrifice their true potential.[45] Perhaps Clarke best summed up these thoughts by pronouncing that a school curriculum should be based upon physiology. The motto of education must be, "educate a man for manhood, a woman for womanhood."[46]

Exaggerated concerns over women's health and actions reinforced another mid-century perceived crisis. At that time (and continuing throughout the century), many medical and popular writers expressed great alarm at what they believed to be a sharply declining American birth rate. The fundamental observation that women in the late nineteenth century bore fewer children was essentially correct. Observers did, however, greatly exaggerate the abruptness of the falling birth rate. Beard, for example, beleved it had dropped over thirty per cent.[47] Contrary to these estimates, the decline did not in fact begin suddenly at mid-century, but instead occurred gradually over a period of more than a hundred years.

Critics viewed this dropping American birth-rate not as the logical or desirable result of social mobility, but as a weakness. Nor did they concede any cooperation on the part of husbands, preferring to view it solely as a women's issue. Many writers traced the declining American birth rate to the struggle of the middle-class women to elevate (or secure) their position.[48] The *Arena* blamed what it saw as an abundance of aging bachelors (those over thirty years of age) on over-ambitious women who had been taught everything at school except their proper roles. Men thus refrained from marrying for fear that they could not support the luxurious tastes of these women. In every large store, the magazine noted, "are to be found numbers of girls who prefer to work outside [the home] in order to dress more finely."[49] Such indulgence would ultimately prove tragic. Soon it would be too late for marriage and only then would many women realize that they had missed the greatest pleasure that life afforded. "Oh! you maids," the article concluded, if such a time comes, "you will be truthful if you place the blame where it belongs, upon yourselves."[50]

The underlying logic of many writers implied that the increasing bad health of American women was simply the fault of the women themselves. Women were sick (and the nation thus imperiled) because they were acting in unwomanly ways. They were in essence failing to be women.[51] By neglecting their homes and pursuing unfeminine goals they violated the physiological laws of nature. Violations of these laws included such things as education, overly fashionable life-styles, suffrage, and birth control.[52] Augustus Gardiner, for example, believed that an overwhelming desire for luxury and fashion had induced many middle-class American women to take various precautionary measures against conception. Such a movement loomed ominous for Gardiner and he stated undeniably that all methods so employed were physically injurious, leading to utter exhaustion or total invalidism. In fact, he maintained, "much of the nervous, hysterical, worn-out, good-for-nothing character of the women of the higher classes" stemmed from the practice of this "thoughtless, ignorant sin against the laws of life and health."[53] The desire for luxury, status, and position, threatened to undermine the very foundations of American society.

Popular Science reminded its readers that Sir Francis Galton had already demonstrated scientifically that a nation could be quietly and effectively wiped out merely by making its women marry at the age of twenty-eight. Beyond that age, the magazine explained, they would not produce enough children (six was the optimum number) to replenish the race.[54] Also writing for *Popular Science*, Dr. A. Lapthorn Smith echoed this view. Smith likewise believed that a woman in her late twenties was too old to raise a family of sufficient size. In much used rhetoric he especially blamed education for "leading women to live an abnormal single life often until age twenty-seven instead of marriage at eighteen," which he claimed was "the latest that nature intended."[55] If this trend were to continue for a prolonged period, the results would prove tragic. According to Clarke, the wives who were to be mothers in this republic would have to be drawn from trans-Atlantic homes.[56]

Charles W. Eliot, president of Harvard University, believed that only a return to wifely duties would cure such illnesses. In an article written for *Ladies' Home Journal* he addressed the "common impression" held by women that to procure intellectual advancement they needed to have occupations or training similar to that of men. He lamented that "the common life of women in bearing and rearing children and making a home for a family is not thought of as affording the wife and mother the means and opportunity for an intellectual development." Such thinking was simply not rational according to Eliot.

Housekeeping and household management, he announced, could in fact provide women with all the mental training they could possibly desire. Especially with the coming of children, there would be many new things to learn and countless opportunities for "careful thought and wisdom." Most certainly, the mother of several children (five or six Eliot thought to be good numbers) would find excellent opportunities for intellectual development. Thus, the "Normal American Woman" not only found fulfillment in traditional housework, but contributed mightily to the real progress of the nation.[57]

Americans seemed to be showing a tragic weakness at an inopportune time. The belief was developing that the thousands of immigrants arriving each year came from debased regions of Europe. When compared to the Anglo-Saxon, they constituted what many observers feared to be a distinctly inferior race drained of all the superior traits which had allowed the American people to build such a great nation.[58] According to Dio Lewis, American society and government had been a success because they had been guided by the Yankee brain. Yet now, fewer children were born to this group. Moreover, many died in infancy and those surviving were not endowed with vigorous health.[59] It was not inconceivable that the very heart of the nation's greatness could die out and its place taken by those of backward origins. America could not grow and prosper dominated by such "stock." In foreboding words, Lewis concluded, "I tremble lest the rudder [of the nation] should fall to hands, which in other lands, have been found utterly incompetent."[60]

Health was thus transformed from a private and personal issue to one of grave national concern. Americans must restore or preserve health, not simply as a duty to God or themselves, but for the preservation of country and race. At the close of the century many onlookers agreed with the findings of prominent New England writer and politician, Prescott Hall, who wrote that if the native element or stock continued to decline amidst such large-scale immigration, America would suffer an irreversible loss of national character.[61]

The debate over women's health revealed a great deal about American social thought and values. The idea that women's health was both dominated and limited by her reproductive system was, in fact, an ancient argument. Yet at no time were those beliefs more entrenched and prevalent than in nineteenth century America.[62] Such medical pronouncements served both to reflect and to reinforce the prevailing conservative view of women's social and domestic role. Experts focused on the theory of women's limited nervous energy and the critical need for it during puberty to sanction attacks on any behavior they deemed unfeminine. They labelled all nontraditional activities as both unwomanly and unnatural, warning that they would produce disease and debility.[63]

Here the overlapping of scientific and cultural theories is quite clear. Gynecology was the weakest link in the already weak armor of the nineteenth century physician's knowledge.[64] As a result, the origin of many theories lay not in empirical data but had deeper roots in cultural beliefs. The resulting arguments against the unwomanly woman often strained credibility. Far from being strictly medical tenets, they were powered by a host of nineteenth century axioms: survival of the fittest, Anglo-Saxonism, race suicide, and the dreams of an orderly society.[65]

All too often, doctors, scholars, and a host of popular writers dealt with the much advertised problem of declining health by directing the blame to American women. The perceived weakness of women made the other threats to American society such as urbanization, industrialization, and immigration loom more ominous. Many observers feared that the nation could only withstand these assaults on stability if its people possessed strength, vitality, and health. Yet by the end of the century, science and medicine had handed down a rather harsh indictment against the American woman. As the nineteenth century continued, however, various writers (many from the field of women's higher education) would take up their pens to exonerate women of these dubious charges.

Chapter Two Notes

1. "Editors' Table: Weariness of the World and its Work," *Godey's Ladies' Book* (May 1860), p. 467.

2. Edward H. Clarke, *Sex in Education; or a Fair Chance for the Girls* (Boston: Rand, Avery, and Co., 1873), reprint ed., Arno Press, 1973, p. 21.

3. Catherine Beecher, *Physiology and Calisthenics for Schools and Families* (New York, 1856), cited in Ann Douglas Wood, "The Fashionable Diseases: Women's Complaints and Their Treatment in Nineteenth Century America," in Mary Hartman, Lois Banner, eds. *Clio's Consciousness Raised. New Perspectives on the History of Women* (New York: Colophon, 1974), p. 2.

4. Dr. Jonathan Stainback Wilson, "Health Department," *Godey's Ladies' Book* (September 1863), pp. 277-278.

5. Dr. Samuel Gregory, "Female Physicians," *Living Age* (May 3, 1862), p. 243.

6. Nancy Oppenheim, *Shattered Nerves, Doctors, Patients, and Depression in Victorian England* (New York: Oxford University Press, 1991), p. 233.

7. Cited in Gail Parker, ed., *The Oven Birds. American Women on Womanhood* (Garden City, New York: Anchor, 1972), p. 177.

8. Edward Youmans, "The Higher Education of Women," *Popular Science* (April 1874), p. 275.

9. Dr. Jonathan Stainback Wilson, "Health Department," *Godey's Ladies' Book* (March 1860), p. 275.

10. "The Health of Our Girls," *Atlantic Monthly* (June 1862), p. 731.

11. Dr. Jonathan Stainback Wilson, "Health Department," *Godey's Ladies' Book* (March 1860), p. 275.

12. *Ibid.*

13. Augustus Kinsley Gardiner, *Conjugal Sins Against the Laws of Life and Health* (New York: J.S. Redfield, 1870), reprint ed., Arno Press, 1974, p. 83.

14. George Beard, *American Nervousness, Its Causes and Consequences* (New York: Putnam's Sons, 1881) reprint ed., Arno Press, 1972, pp. 94-95; see also Arvilla B. Haynes, M.D., "Lecture IV," in Abba Woolson, ed., *Dress Reform: A Series of Lectures Delivered in Boston on Dress as it Effects the Health of Women* (Boston: Roberts Brothers, 1874), reprint ed., Arno Press, 1974, pp. 119-120.

15. Mary Sanford-Blake, M.D., "Lecture I," in Woolson, ed., *Dress Reform*, p. 15.

16. Wilson, "Health Department," *Godey's Ladies' Book* (March 1860), p. 275.

17. "Wet Nurses," *Godey's Ladies' Book* (July 1860), p. 80.

18. Beard, *American Nervousness*, pp. 77-78.

19. *Ibid.*

20. Edward H. Dixon, M.D., *Woman and Her Diseases, From the Cradle to the Grave: Adapted Exclusively to Her Instruction in the Physiology of Her System, and all the Diseases of Her Critical Periods* 10th ed., (Philadelphia: G.G. Evans, 1860), p. 237.

21. Janice Golden, "From Wet-Nurse Directory to Milk Bank: The Delivery of Human Milk in Boston," *Bulletin of the History of Medicine* (Winter 1988), p. 592.

22. "Wet-Nurses," *Godey's Ladies' Book* (July 1860), p. 81.

23. *Ibid.*

24. Wood, "The Fashionable Diseases," p. 3; See also, Carroll Smith-Rosenberg, "Puberty to Menopause: The Cycle of Femininity in Nineteenth Century America," in Hartman and Banner, eds., *Clio's Consciousness Raised*, p. 26.

25. John Wiltbank, *Introductory Lecture for the Session, 1853-54* (Philadelphia: Edward Grattan, 1854), p. 7, cited in Smith-Rosenberg, "Puberty to Menopause," p. 24.

26. Cited in Wood, "The Fashionable Diseases," p. 3.

27. *Ibid.*

28. Cited in Smith-Rosenberg, "Puberty to Menopause," p. 25.

29. Clarke, *Sex in Education*, pp. 22, 90.

30. *Ibid.*, p. 40-41.

31. Lousie Michelle Newman, *Men's Ideas/ Men's Realities, Popular Science, 1870-1915* (New York: Pergamon Press, 1985), p. 106.

32. Larry Owens, "Pure and Sound Government. Laboratories, Playing Fields, and Gymnasia in the Nineteenth Century Search for Order," *Isis* (June 1985), p. 189.

33. Clarke, *Sex in Education*, p. 42.

34. Smith-Rosenberg, "Puberty to Menopause," p. 2.

35. "The Health of Our Girls," *Atlantic Monthly*, (June 1862), p. 724.

36. Clarke, *Sex in Education*, p. 18.

37. Nathalie Dana, *Young in New York, A Memoir of a Victorian Girlhood* (Garden City, New York: Doubleday, 1962), p. 79.

38. Clarke, *Sex in Education*, pp. 39, 61-62, 116.

39. *Ibid.*, pp. 92-93.

40. E. Lynn Linton, "The Revolt Against Matrimony," *Forum* (January 1891), p. 588.

41. John S. Billings, "The Diminishing Birth-Rate in the United States," *Forum* (June 1893), p. 475. See also, Thomas Bentzon, "Family Life in America," *Forum* (March 1896), pp. 11-12.

42. Wood, "The Fashionable Diseases," p. 29.

43. Lewis, *Our Girls* (New York: Harper and Brothers, 1871), p. 11.

44. Youmans, "The Higher Education of Women," *Popular Science* (April 1874), p. 750.

45. Grant Allen, "Plain Words on the Woman Question," *Popular Science* (December 1889), p. 178.

46. Clarke, *Sex in Education*, pp. 18-19.

47. Beard, *American Nervousness*, p. 79.

48. For an outstanding analysis of middle-class aspirations and behavior, see Harvey Levenstein, *Revolution at the Table, The Transformation of the American Diet* (New York: Oxford University Press, 1980).

49. Henry Waldorf Francis,"Marriage and Dress," *Arena* (March 1902), p. 292-293.

50. *Ibid.*, p. 296.

51. Wood, "The Fashionable Diseases," p. 43.

52. Smith-Rosenberg, "Puberty to Menopause," p. 30.

53. Gardiner, *Conjugal Sins*, pp. 117, 178, 229.

54. Grant Allen, "Plain Words on the Woman Question," *Popular Science* (December 1889), p. 173.

55. A. Lapthorn Smith, M.D., "Higher Education of Women and Race Suicide," *Popular Science* (December 1889), p. 173.

56. Clarke, *Sex in Education*, p. 63.

57. Charles W. Eliot, "The Normal American Woman," *Ladies' Home Journal* (January 1908), p. 1.

58. The most complete discussion of such racial theories remains, John Higham, *Strangers in the Land, Patterns of American Nativism, 1860-1925* (New York: Atheneum, 1971).

59. Lewis, *Our Girls*, p. 11.

60. *Ibid.*, pp. 10-11.

61. Prescott Hall, *Immigration and its Effect Upon the United States* (New York: Holt and Co., 1906), p. 35.

62. Newman, *Men's Ideas/ Women's Realities*, p. 24.

63. Smith-Rosenberg, "Puberty to Menopause," pp. 27, 33.

64. Wood, "The Fashionable Diseases," p. 32.

65. Janice Law Trecker, "Sex, Science, and Education," *American Quarterly* (October 1974), pp. 353-355.

CHAPTER THREE

In Defense of Womanhood: Exercise as Cure and Preventative

Medical and popular writers alike spilled much ink depicting American women as weak and diseased. Yet, it should be noted that such pronouncements were not limited to male writers. Similar logic permeated the writings of many prominent women authors as well. For example, Virginia Penny, writing for *Ladies' Repository* in 1865, stated that ill-health in America was "fast becoming proverbial." After long consideration she had concluded that the problem posed by the "tender and fragile nature of American women" was very real and threatening and could not be dismissed as mere myth.[1] Even the *Woman's Journal,* a major voice of the suffrage movement, echoed this sentiment. In a 1873 article, the magazine confirmed that the health of women was deteriorating from one generation to the next, and as a result, "the sons of such mothers would suffer."[2]

By far, the most eloquent voice on this subject belonged to the early women's activist, Catherine Beecher. Beecher had long been interested in the issue of women's health. In 1835 (at the age of thirty-five), she suffered a nervous breakdown. Before her death in 1878, she had visited no less than thirteen different health establishments. Her conclusions were remarkably pessimistic. She wrote in 1871 that the more she travelled, the more she was convinced that there existed a "terrible decay of female health all over the land...increasing in a most alarming ratio." To support her findings she noted that out of twenty-three of her married sisters, sisters-in-law, and female cousins, twenty were either delicate or invalid. In all of Boston, Beecher could think of only one married friend who enjoyed perfect health. She grimly concluded that among her "immense circle of friends and acquaintances all over the Union," she could count only ten married women who were in sound health.[3]

While perhaps sharing the observation that sickness was widespread, many writers offered an entirely different prognosis than that given by experts such as Dr. Clarke. In stirring rhetoric, these authors assailed the belief that women were, by their very nature, feeble. This concept was central to their arguments, for if it could be demonstrated that the perceived weakness of women was not an inescapable part of nature's design, then the condition could be remedied.

Dr. Mercy Jackson wrote that she could not follow the logic of medical writers, especially Clarke, who portrayed women as innately flawed. According to Jackson, Clarke seemed to impugn the wisdom of God. Surely, she theorized, the Almighty "knew how to make women." He would most certainly not, therefore, create a weak or enfeebled being upon whom the race depended.[4] If women did not appear well, it was not, as Clarke and other critics had stated, because of how nature had made them, but rather because of how they had made themselves. The true cause of sickness must be identified and then corrected. As Dr. Arvilla Haynes described, sickness was in fact an unnatural state, brought about by "a perversion of the natural functions, and a disregard of hygienic laws."[5]

Having announced that women were not destined to weakness, defenders of womanhood busied themselves explaining the various causes of ill-health among women. Dio Lewis proclaimed that women's health problems stemmed from a lack of exercise in childhood. Exercise, as Lewis often repeated, was "the great law of development." Yet girls failed to take any. More accurately stated, they were allowed none.[6] In an earlier day, girls ran around more, played more, and as a result grew up more robust. But now, changes in social customs had destroyed the opportunity for such healthful exercise.[7] Lewis bitterly complained that according to current fashion, the fragile and pale girl was thought by "many silly people" to be more of a lady than one with ruddy cheeks and vigorous health. They associated a strong muscular body with the working class (servants most notably) while insisting that true ladies should appear sickly and pale.[8] To instill such ladylike gentility, parents often confined their girls to the house. There, shut off from fresh air and healthful exercise, they sadly deteriorated. It was no wonder then, Lewis noted, that these girls grew up weak.

They were not allowed to do anything to strengthen their muscles or tone their nerves.[9]

Godey's Ladies' Book also took a strong stand on this subject, proclaiming that exercise restored health and strength.[10] It especially praised exercise for girls as a means of promoting health and developing strength and vigor. *Godey's* found it incredible that so many girls could be "willing to sit thus idly from day to day having so little exercise...wasting their energies in comparative idleness and consequently suffering in their health." Such girls eventually became habitual invalids, whether real or fancied. Many became so enfeebled that they fell prey to lung diseases such as consumption.[11]

Godey's staff medical writer, Dr. Jonathan Stainback Wilson, boldly announced that women should submit to no restraints in the area of health. No false sense of gentility or unreasonable subservience to public opinion should deter any woman from engaging in sports or exercises that would develop her lungs. Health should never be hindered by fashion. There would always be, Wilson noted, that "brainless set of fools and simpering jackdaws who would sacrifice life to a shoe buckle" if fashion demanded. The "daughters of the heroes of '76" should, however, sternly resist any tampering with their health and well-being.[12] In equally strong language, another *Godey's* author wrote to her women readers, "you are ruining yourself...take exercise." Vigorous walks were always in order. Even a run would not destroy the dignity of character. Women should "sit less, and stand, run, jump, and frolic more."[13]

Although the "close confinement of city life" did in small part limit opportunities for health-bestowing exercise, it was but a small obstacle. In addition to vigorous walks, *Godey's* suggested that those women living in cities could exercise by running up stairs, provided that they did so with their mouths closed.[14] Breathing through the nose would purify the air, arrest the passage of small insects and dust particles, and prevent "the inhalation of poisonous gases." It also served as a natural safeguard against overexertion, for if one were compelled to breathe through the mouth, the exercise was obviously too strenuous.[15]

Having attacked the stereotypical pale and fragile woman, popular writers faced their next obstacles. They must quiet any fears that exercise would coarsen the upper classes or strip young ladies of their feminine charm and social standing. *Godey's* assured its readers that their girls would suffer no loss of status if they exercised. Such action, they maintained was now quite common among the upper classes of Europe. In Berlin, for example, exclusive schools taught swimming to all "high-bred young ladies." Such physical training built health, strength, and grace of figure and character.[16]

Writers used various tactics in reconciling the passive notion of true womanhood with the dynamic image of physical exercise. A common argument stated that physical training would not destroy femininity but would rather fulfill its greater potential. Popular showman Eugene Sandow scoffed at the idea that exercise would make boys out of young girls. Quite the contrary, he claimed, exercise would develop the "grace of form and beauty of outline" that would make girls even more attractive to men.[17] Writing for the *Atlantic Monthly* in 1861, the author of "Gymnastics" was also explicit concerning the benefits of exercise. He claimed to have known "an invalid girl so lame from childhood that she could not stand without support." Through the practice of gymnastics, her health was restored and her "bust and arms made a study for a sculptor."[18]

By promoting beauty, exercise would render great service to girls and make them more, not less, feminine. *Godey's* concluded that if more young ladies would take exercise there would be no need for face paints or powders. Cheeks would then be naturally fresh and rosy, and complexions soft, clear, and beautiful.[19] In fact, the magazine claimed, "many a case of chronic ugliness might be cured through the means of healthy exercise."[20]

For many writers the most formidable obstacle to any health reform for women was the prevailing style of dress. Dress reform, therefore, became a major movement closely associated with any campaign for women's health. Women's fashions interfered with attempts to improve the health of women in many ways. First, the heavy and restrictive clothing impeded movement and made any form of exercise nearly impossible. The *Atlantic Monthly* noted that some system of physical training was greatly needed, but without dress reform, no progress could be made. The magazine complained that "the present mode of [women's] dress" interfered with "the ease and physiological benefits of exercise." Simply stated, a fashionably dressed woman could not possibly exercise.[21]

Dress reform advocate Dr. Mercy Jackson reported in 1874 that the present style of clothing (especially narrow shoes) disabled women to such a degree that not one woman in twenty could walk at all without complete exhaustion.[22] Jackson's colleague, Dr. Mary Sanford Blake, concurred noting that prescribing exercise for ladies availed them nothing, "pinched and burdened as they are." Anyone hampered by their clothing in such a manner would naturally seek "a level of muscular inactivity."[23]

Women's clothing also conspired against health in a far more sinister manner. According to some critics, it actually caused disease. Many observers quickly singled out one garment, the corset, as the chief agent of disease and debility. Indeed, the incidence of chlorosis (a commonly diagnosed form of anemia produced by iron deficiency and aggravated by the loss of menstrual blood) seemed to parallel the practice of tight lacing which began in the 1850s and rose to the level of high fashion in the 1860s and 1870s.[24] *Godey's* contributing medical writer, Dr. Charles P. Uhle, wrote that he regarded the corset as the one relic of barbarism still existing among American women.[25] The garment by constricting the chest and waist impeded all the major internal organs. Uhle claimed that the compression of the lungs and liver meant that blood was neither aerated nor purified properly. A woman so attired suffered from slow bowels, irritated nerves, hysteria, and fainting. Furthermore, she could not nurse a baby and stood in constant peril from lung diseases. Speaking for the magazine, Uhle pronounced that "we look upon the practice as an inexcusable and abominable one and believe that a more indefensible sin against the laws of health does not exist upon the face of the civilized earth."[26]

Corsets also aggravated the chlorotic tendency in a more mundane manner. By purely mechanical pressure the devices must have decreased the volume of food ingested. Additionally the quest for the perfect hourglass figure was an unquestionably strong inducement for women to restrict their dietary intake to an unsafe level.[27]   This situation was complicated by the strong nineteenth century belief that foods derived from animals increased the sexual appetite.   As a result, many women further limited their iron ingestion by eschewing meat, eggs, and even milk.[28] Dress reformers also warned that the sheer volume of a proper woman's clothing could inflict injury. Dr. Uhle railed against what he termed "the loads of skirts" suspended from the waist. He contended that the very weight of these garments (estimated by some historians at an average of thirty-seven pounds per outfit), produced a continuous strain upon the muscles of the back and abdomen.[29]   In addition to its weight, fashionable dress threatened health by keeping some parts of the body too warm and other parts too cold. If one area of the body were cold, the theory went, it would be deprived of its normal quantity of warmth-giving blood. Consequently, another body area must then have more than its normal supply, thus causing congestion. Fashion, it appeared to health advocates, conspired to keep the extremities cold (through low necklines, thin shoes, and light stockings) while the lungs and especially the uterine organs were liable to congestions. According to some medical observers, such a predicament would prove critical for girls during puberty. Exposure to cold (with its corresponding overheating of the internal organs) at that age often produced "derangements" that in later life became chronic.[30]

Godey's claimed that such destructive fashions were a peculiarly American phenomenon. The author of an editorial entitled "Swedish Women" mentioned that in his travels he had never seen a low-necked dress or a thin shoe in Stockholm. There, women dressed for comfort and health, not for style or ornament. "I protest, I lose all patience," he penned furiously, "when I think of the habits of our American Women." He concluded that "if ever the Saxon race does deteriorate on the American side of the Atlantic, as some ethnologists anticipate, it will be wholly their [American women] fault."[31] In addition to Sweden, other nations were presented as examples of good health, including Switzerland, Austria, and especially England.[32]

Unfortunately for health reformers, fashion did not crumble before such sharp rhetoric. The corset occupied such a prominent place in women's clothing that many of its critics despaired. Uhle admitted that no well-dressed woman of any age could be found whose chest was not "laced and bound even though the practice was killing her inch by inch." He was especially galled by the mothers who wrote asking when they should first put corsets on their daughters. His favorite reply was a caustic, "When I put them on my horse."[33]

Some pessimistic health advocates believed that grown women were sadly beyond reform. Set in their ways, they were both slaves to fashion and to the tyranny of the corset. Dr. Caroline Hastings reasoned that a woman over eighteen years of age would very likely believe that she could not live without her corset. After all, her muscles had never been allowed to support the spine or abdomen. When forced to do so in the absence of the rigid corset, these muscles routinely failed.[34]

With despair, many health reformers turned their attention away from the adult woman. Perhaps younger girls could be taught the proper habits which their mothers might not adopt. Eventually, these changes in dress, diet, and exercise would bring about remarkable improvements in women's health. Mary T. Bissell, an 1881 graduate of Women's Medical College, predicted that if outdoor life were ever made available and attractive to girls, great changes would follow. When people accepted that "a nobly developed and active body" was the daughter's birthright as well as the son's, chronic ill-health among women would end.[35]

Proponents of women's education quickly seized on these arguments. If the apparent invalidism of women could be explained as the result of idleness, improper dress, or lack of exercise, then education could be cleared of the charges levelled against it by critics such as Clarke. *Godey's Ladies' Book*, a staunch supporter of women's colleges, wrote in 1874 that they were exceedingly glad that a new book had been written in reply to Clarke's *Sex in Education*. According to the magazine, the authors of this book directly attacked Clarke's position, "assailed him fearlessly, fought prejudice with logic, and in brief demolished him entirely."[36] Colleges and schools simply could not be blamed for the general ill-health of women. In a sharply worded address, Abba Woolson stated that doctors who attributed the "sad decay of our young women" to excessive study were ignorant. The problem was not that boys and girls were trained too much alike mentally, but rather that they were trained too little alike physically. The solution, then, was not to enfeeble women's minds by denying them education, but instead to strengthen their bodies.[37]

For guidance in this area, many college administrators turned to an early pioneer in the field of physical training, Dio Lewis. Lewis, a long-standing advocate of such causes as temperance and women's rights, as well as health reform, had studied gymnastics while in Europe during the 1850s. In 1861, he began physical training classes in Boston convinced that such exercises could lead to health reform.[38] Unlike some of his colleagues, Lewis included women in his classes. His system centered upon three principles: adequate ventilation, light exercise, and loose clothing. He strictly forbade corsets so that women could move about "with perfect liberty about the waist." The program itself consisted of stretching movements, light dumbbell exercises, and isometric presses. Additionally, a series of throwing and catching exercises (with bean bags) rounded out the system providing, Lewis believed, hand-eye coordination as well as "coolness of nerve."[39]

Lewis advertised great results. At his Lexington Normal School, his regimen of "new gymnastics", warm flannel, sturdy shoes, and the ban on corsets had vanquished female weakness. Lewis claimed that his students left the school on average three inches greater across the chest, free from aches, and "nobly fitted for the grave responsibilities of citizenship and motherhood."[40] As a result of Lewis's writings, many proponents of women's education believed that gymnastics (or at least some program of "well-regulated bodily exercise") would furnish the proper health safeguards.[41] In 1862, the trustees of Mount Holyoke sent two faculty members to Boston for a three week course of study with Lewis. At that time the college actually had its own exercise program based upon housework and light calisthenics. The calisthenics, however, had proven unpopular with the students. Additionally, many critics had raised considerable objections to the exercises on the grounds that they resembled dancing too closely.[42] Lewis especially opposed dancing, believing that with its "peculiar contact" between the man and woman, it led to impure thoughts and often served as an excuse for gross indelicacy. Even female-only dances done as exercises at some schools raised his ire, because as Lewis explained, the rotary motion would prove injurious to the brain and spinal marrow.[43]

With great regularity the numerous women's colleges that opened during the latter part of the nineteenth century adopted similar programs. For example, the 1865 Vassar College catalog announced that "the system of Light Gymnastics, as perfected by Dr. Dio Lewis will be taught to all the College without extra charge." Each student would, however, be required to provide her own "light and easy-fitting dress adapted to these exercises."[44] Similarly, the Wellesley College catalog of 1876 also proclaimed that good health was absolutely essential to good scholarship. The college urged the public to note that the "prevailing ill-health of American school-girls" was not due to hard study, but rather to "the violation of the plain laws of nature." Such a condition was easily remedied with the proper amounts of fresh air, suitable dress, and sufficient daily exercise.[45]

In addition to gymnastics, many colleges adopted remedial programs. At Bryn Mawr, for example, students received a thorough examination before being assigned to gymnasium work and those students needing any corrective exercises were then assigned to special classes. All other students performed two hours of general indoor gymnastics each week as well as two hours of outdoor recreation.[46] Mount Holyoke also formed special physical training classes for students otherwise unfit for basic gymnastics. The college described the results of such remedial training as "marvelously encouraging." Now, many students who previously had been excused from gymnasium work (mostly because of spinal curvatures or weak arches) received corrective therapy.[47]

Vassar College trustees also promised to build and protect the health of their students, but in an appropriate manner. Accordingly, physical training at Vassar would be carefully administered by a woman professor and would include only those activities "suitable for ladies...and promotive of bodily strength and grace."[48] In general, the entire curriculum was to be completely womanly with nothing unfeminine tolerated in the instruction given to students. For example, the trustees and president did not view "oratory and debate" as feminine accomplishments and consequently such a course was not offered. The intellectual course of study would be "ample but not crushing" and would include "Domestic Sciences." *Godey's* was very pleased to hear this plan. They had long complained that "home duties" had never been made a "theme of honor and importance in schools for young ladies," and as a result, education too often led women to disdain the household.[49]

Domestic science and physical training overlapped. A woman could not fulfill her duties if not in vigorous health, and consequently Vassar students also received instruction on such topics as nutrition, hygiene, and bathing.[50] Similarly, Mount Holyoke professors attempted to introduce a few personal hygiene lectures into the regular physiology course. The lectures on the female reproductive organs caused such a storm of protest that eventually the college cancelled all instruction in anatomy and physiology.[51]

With remarkable speed, women's colleges brought about a startling reversal in popular thought. The various physical education programs, by both building and preserving health, seemed to prove that women were not naturally feeble. Bryn Mawr's president, M. Carey Thomas could proudly proclaim that although once considered invalids, college women could now be presented as the very models of female health.[52] In 1886, the *Forum* announced that the establishment of women's colleges had generated enough proof that Clarke was wrong. Mental application, with the proper food and exercise, did not injure the health of women. Quite the contrary, it improved it. The vigorous alumnae from Vassar, Wellesley, and Smith had shown conclusively that college-trained women were healthier than their non-collegiate counterparts. The magazine went as far as to quantify its claims, stating that recent investigations had proven that "among college graduates, there is a gain of twenty-two percent upon the health of the average woman."[53]

The colleges themselves served as excellent sources of their own quantitative publicity. Wellesley College, for example, advertised that their physical education classes had produced impressive results. Specifically, students there showed a gain of nearly two inches across the chest, eight inches across the shoulders, and an increase of twenty-one pounds of strength in the back.[54] Exercise very quickly established itself as the prerequisite for health in college. Writing in *Munsey's Magazine* in 1901, Anne O'Hagan stated plainly that no women's college would even think of sending out a catalog that did not contain "alluring pictures of its gymnasium."[55]

Advocates of women's education did not stand alone in their praise of female fitness. Here educational concerns combined with the native-white-Protestant preoccupation with health and the presumably declining birth rate. Many observers saw the well-managed gymnasium as a means of assuring the biological future of the nation.[56] This group readily accepted the role of exercise in college. There, it provided the "young girls who will be the mothers of tomorrow a fine safety valve that prevents the top of their head from blowing off with the pressure of high-brow studies."[57] Yet physical training would serve other purposes. Edwyn Sandys, for example, claimed that exercise programs for women would increase fertility and strengthen women for childbearing. He believed that "the out-door girl of today" was clearly "the queen of her sex" and would be the mother "of a race of stalwarts of the future," and thus the race would be perpetuated.[58]

Advocates of this view further added to the already conservative nature of physical education for women. Educators had promised that college would not change women, but would instead make them better. It would elevate women, not to change their place in the home, but to train them for the "high and noble duties of life." Through physical training, women would be saved from ill-health, not to escape their traditional roles, but rather to become better wives and mothers.[59]

Some historians have noted that in analyzing women and sport, the tendency has been to treat women as the variable and sport as a constant. In truth, both underwent considerable change.[60] As the nineteenth century closed, the role of sporting activities remained much smaller than it would be in future decades. True sports for women, aside from gymnastics or calisthenics, were just beginning their evolution. Many young women may well have received their first introduction to exercise in schools and colleges, but still, the emergence of a true sporting woman would await a future day.

Chapter Three Notes

1. Virginia Penny, "Poor Health of American Women," *Ladies' Repository* (March 1865), p. 155.

2. "Artificial Disabilities," *Woman's Journal* (January 4, 1873), p. 2.

3. Cited in Gail Parker, ed., *The Oven Birds, American Women on Womanhood, 1820-1920* (Garden City, New York: Anchor Books, 1972), pp. 145-146, 167-174.

4. Cited in Julia Ward Howe, *Sex and Education, A Reply to Dr. E.H. Clarke's Sex in Education* (Boston: Roberts Brothers, 1874), reprint ed., Arno Press, 1972, pp. 155-156.

5. Arvilla B. Haynes, M.D., "Lecture IV," in Abba Woolson, ed., *Dress Reform: A Series of Lectures Delivered in Boston on Dress as it Affects the Health of Women* (Boston: Roberts Brothers, 1874), p. 98.

6. Dio Lewis, *Our Girls* (New York: Harper and Brothers, 1871), p. 92.

7. *Ibid.* See also, "Editors' Table: The Physical Training of Girls," *Godey's Ladies' Book* (November 1870), p. 471; "The Health of Our Girls," *Atlantic Monthly* (June 1862), p. 723.

8. Lewis, *Our Girls*, pp. 66, 69.

9. *Ibid.*, p. 103.

10. "Country Life and its Advantages," *Godey's Ladies' Book* (October 1860), pp. 366-367.

11. "Hints About Health," *Godey's Ladies' Book* (July 1867), p. 80. See also "Death In-Doors," *Godey's Ladies' Book* (November 1867), p. 449.

12. Dr. Jonathan Stainback Wilson, "Health Department," *Godey's Ladies' Book* (January 1860), p. 82.

13. "Early Rising and Exercise," *Godey's Ladies' Book* (October 1864), p. 222. See also, "Exercise for Girls," *Godey's Ladies' Book* (July 1867), pp. 80-81.

14. "Hints About Health," *Godey's Ladies' Book* (September 1866), pp. 263-264.

15. "Hints About Health." *Godey's Ladies' Book* (June 1867), p. 559.

16. "Editors' Table," *Godey's Ladies' Book* (April 1860), pp. 369-370.

17. G. Mercer Adam, ed., *Sandow on Physical Training, A Study in Perfect Form* (New York: Selwin Tait and Sons, 1894), pp. 154-155.

18. "Gymnastics," *Atlantic Monthly* (March 1861), p. 299.

19. Dr. Charles P. Uhle, "Face Powders and Paints," *Godey's Ladies' Book* (February 1869), p. 189.

20. "Early Rising and Exercise," *Godey's Ladies' Book* (October 1864), p. 322.

21. "Weak Lungs and How to Make Them Strong," *Atlantic Monthly* (June 1863), p. 669.

22. Mercy Jackson, M.D., "Lecture III," in Woolson, ed., *Dress Reform*, p. 75.

23. Mary J. Sanford-Blake, M.D., "Lecture I," in Woolson ed., *Dress Reform* pp. 22-23.

24. Robert P. Hudson, "The Biography of a Disease: Lessons from Chlorosis," *Bulletin of the History of Medicine* (March 1977), p. 458.

25. Dr. Charles P. Uhle, "Health Department," *Godey's Ladies' Book* (March 1869), p. 283.

26. Dr. Charles P. Uhle, "Health Department," *Godey's Ladies' Book* (June 1872), pp. 575-576.

27. Hudson, "The Biography of a Disease," pp. 457-458.

28. *Ibid.*

29. Dr. Charles P. Uhle, "Health Department," *Godey's Ladies' Book* (March 1869), p. 28. See also Barbara Ehrenreich and Deidre English, *For Her Own Good, One Hundred Years of the Experts' Advice to Women* (New York: Anchor Press, 1978), p. 98.

30. Arvilla B. Haynes, "Lecture III," in Woolson ed., *Dress Reform*, pp. 117-118.

31. "Editors' Table,"" *Godey's Ladies' Book* (June 1860), p. 559.

32. "The Health of Our Girls," *Atlantic Monthly* (June 1862), pp. 722-723; Augustus Kinsley Gardiner, *Conjugal Sins Against the Laws of Life and Health* (New York: J.S. Redfield, 1870), reprint ed., Arno Press, 1974, p. 212; Lewis, *Our Girls, p. 184;* "The Health and Physical Habits of English and American Women," *Scribners' Monthly* (April 1874), p. 747; George Beard, *American Nervousness, Its Causes and Consequences* (New York: Putnam's Sons, 1881), pp. 33-42; John Habberton, "Open-Air Recreation for Women," *Outing* (November 1885), p. 160; Elizabeth Bisland, "Famous Beauties," *Cosmopolitan* (September 1896), p. 632; Elizabeth Barney, "The American Sportswoman," *Fortnightly Review* (August 1, 1899), p. 263.

33. Dr. Charles P. Uhle, "Health Department," *Godey's Ladies' Book* (March 1869), p. 283.

34. Caroline Hastings, M.D., "Lecture II," in Woolson, ed., *Dress Reform*, p. 49.

35. Mary T. Bissell, "Emotions Versus Health in Women," *Popular Science* (February 1888), cited in Louise Michelle-Newman, *Men's Ideas/ Women's Realities, Popular Science, 1870-1915* (New York: Pergamon Press, 1985), pp. 48, 52.

36. "Literary Notes," *Godey's Ladies' Book* (August 1874), p. 190.

37. Abba Woolson, "Lecture V," in Woolson ed., *Dress Reform*, pp. 175-178.

38. Harvey Green, *Fit for America, Health Fitness, Sport, and American Society* (New York: Pantheon, 1986), p. 184.

39. *Ibid.*, pp. 187-188.

40. Lewis, *Our Girls*, pp. 360-361.

41. "Editors' Table," *Godey's Ladies' Book* (November 1870), p. 471.

42. Persis Harlow McCurdy, "The Physical Training at Mount Holyoke College," *American Physical Education Review* (March 1909), pp. 143-146.

43. Lewis, *Our Girls*, pp. 226, 229.

44. Thomas Woody, *A History of Education in the United States* (New York: Science Press, 1929), p. 118. Woody cites from the 1865-1866 Vassar College Catalog, p. 28.

45. *Ibid.*, p. 121. Woody cites from the 1876-1877 Wellesley College Catalog, pp. 19-20. For more recent works on the subject see especially, Barbara M. Solomon, *In the Company of Educated Women: A History of Women and Higher Education in America* (New Haven: Yale University Press, 1985); Helen Lefkowitz Horowitz, *Alma Mater: Design and Experience in the Women's Colleges from their Nineteenth Century Beginnings to the 1930s* (New York: Knopf, 1984).

46. Elizabeth Paine, "Athletics at Women's Colleges. Smith, Mount Holyoke, Bryn Mawr," *Illustrated Sporting News* (July 9, 1909), p. 148.

47. McCurdy, "The History of Physical Training at Mount Holyoke College," *American Physical Education Review* (March 1909), p. 148.

48. "Editor's Table: Vassar College Opened," *Godey's Ladies' Book* (August 1865), p. 173.

49. *Ibid.*

50. Betty Spears, "The Emergence of Women in Sport," in Barbara J. Hoepner, ed., *Women's Athletics: Coping with Controversy* (Washington, D.C.: AAHPER Publications, 1974), pp. 28-29.

51. McCurdy, "The History of Training at Mount Holyoke College," *American Physical Education Review* (March 1909), p. 149.

52. M. Carey Thomas, "Present Tendencies in Women's College and University Education," *Educational Review* 35 (1908), p. 69.

53. Ella C. Lapham, "Women's Duty to Women," *Forum* (July 1886), p. 461. See also Charlotte Porter, "Physical Hindrances to Teaching Girls," *Forum* (September 1891), p. 41.

54. Nellie Hattan Britan, "Physical Education, What it is Doing for Women," *Education* 29 (1908), p. 38.

55. Anne O'Hagan, "The Athletic Girl," *Munsey's Magazine* (August 1901), p. 733.

56. Donald J. Mrozek, *Sport and American Mentality, 1880-1910* (Knoxville: University of Tennessee Press, 1983), p. 145.

57. J. Nilsen Laurvik, "The American Girl Out-of-Doors," *Woman's Home Companion* (August 1912), p. 18.

58. Edwyn Sandys, "The Place that Women Occupy in Sport," *The Illustrated Sporting News* (November 21, 1903), p. 11.

59. "Editors' Table: Vassar," *Godey's Ladies' Book* (August 1866), p. 170.

60. Mrozek, *Sport and American Mentality*, p. 136.

CHAPTER FOUR

Redefining Health: A Preview of the Sportswoman

By the late nineteenth century, physical education occupied an important position in women's higher education. It had won much acclaim as a builder of health and vitality and had established a recognized safeguard against the perceived strains of higher learning. It was still, however, in its infancy and would change greatly over the next few decades. The closing years of the nineteenth century witnessed a clear and distinct evolution in physical education for women. As American society became more structured and professionalized, physical education also became more formal and sophisticated. It also changed markedly in scope and content with the introduction of sports and games into the college curriculum.

The gymnastics of the 1870s bore little resemblance to the organized and professional physical education programs of the 1900s. Originally, the word gymnasium did not even refer to a whole building given over to physical education. It merely indicated the place where gymnastics were taught. In women's colleges such a place could be any building with sufficient space for calisthenics. Mount Holyoke, for example, employed a storeroom over the coal shed for gymnastics until building a formal gymnasium. Vassar students performed their gymnastics in the wide corridors of Main Hall until their gymnasium was constructed.[1]

Physical education would eventually evolve into a highly structured profession, mirroring the transformation taking place across the nation. From its mid-point on, the nineteenth century witnessed the remarkable emergence of middle-class professionals. Their success depended upon performing a growing number of specialized and novel tasks which a progressive civilization defined as essential. Special rituals and rites of passage such as graduate schools, internships, and bar exams controlled entry into the new professions. The more elaborate the ritual, the more imposing was its symbolic authority. The professions promoted their own national visibility through professional affiliations, journals, and research. Additionally, they policed their own ranks by means of licensing regulations.[2]

Physical education did not escape the growing professionalization of American culture. Its practitioners claimed that as physical training became more of a "science" it should not be taught on a part-time basis or by a faculty member from another department. Consequently, starting in the 1880s, many women's college began establishing independent departments of physical education. (see Table 1.)

Table 1.[3]
Establishment of Physical Education Departments in Colleges

College	Founding Year	P.E. Dep't. Established
Wellesley	1876	1881
Vassar	1865	1883
Bryn Mawr	1885	1885
Smith	1875	1887
Goucher	1888	1888
Mount Holyoke	1837	1891
Radcliffe	1879	1892
Rockford	1849	1892
Mills	1871	1899
Wells	1868	1909
Elmira	1855	1914
Barnard	1889	1918

The situation at Mount Holyoke is an interesting case in point. When the administration announced its desire that the physical education instructor devote more time to teaching and to careful record taking, the instructor, Cornelia Clapp, balked. In addition to her fifteen year stint in gymnastics, Clapp also served as the school's zoology professor. She complained that any increased physical education duties would prove too time consuming and would seriously interfere with her other research. As zoology was the field in which she wished to make her reputation, she wrote to the president of the college in 1891 stating that in her judgment, the time had come for a formal department of physical training, headed by a full-time teacher trained in the "new schools of physical culture." In the fall such a department opened.[4]

Soon physical education sported many of the trappings of a structured profession. In 1895, the American Physical Education Association was formed and began publishing a journal, the *American Physical Education Review*. Physical education was travelling far beyond simple gymnastics, and the profession's leadership maintained that only trained experts should be allowed to teach it. Earlier, there were few schools to train physical educators. But by late century, Wellesley College, Teachers College of Columbia University, and the University of Chicago (along with the normal schools of Dio Lewis and Dudley Sargent) all provided a bountiful supply of diploma-wielding experts. Consequently, by the early years of the twentieth century the professionalization of "gymnastics" was progressing rapidly in the hands of specially trained professionals operating out of independent departments and conducting work in their own facilities.

This trend toward professionalization coincided with another and quite opposite movement in women's physical education. Beginning late in the nineteenth century and continuing into the first years of the next century, a distinct change occurred in many women's physical training regimens. Emphasis began to shift from strict and formal gymnastics toward participation in games and sports. This transition continued until sport became an integral, if not dominant component of most physical education programs. The rise of sport on the campuses of women's colleges provided a great irony. At a time in which physical educators were establishing their professional identity, sports sprang up more spontaneously, often free from professional supervision. Available information indicates that students developed sporting activities long before a place was found for them in the official curriculum.

Because of its "unofficial origins," little is known about the unfolding of sports in women's programs. What information exists, however, is very revealing. In 1897, for example, Sophia Foster Richardson wrote an article for *Popular Science* detailing her experience as a student at Vassar. She reported that twenty years earlier (when she was a freshman), a favorite activity of Vassar students was baseball. So many students played the sport that "seven or eight baseball clubs sprang up spontaneously." Tennis, a more conventional sport, soon gained a greater following and continued to "maintain a hold upon the students." Richardson further wrote that the public was shocked by what little it knew of such activity. Yet by and large, the campus was isolated from public view allowing Vassar students in the "retired grounds and protected from observation by sheltering trees to play in spite of a censorious public."[5]

Official physical education department literature is mostly silent on the issue of student sport participation. Nevertheless, it is obvious that the colleges gave sports their tacit support. Long before these activities were mentioned in college catalogues as part of the physical education program, descriptions of the buildings and grounds clearly show that provisions had been made for them. For example, Goucher College built its pool in 1888, yet the first mention of swimming in statements concerning physical education did not appear until 1904.[6] Similarly, the *Calendar of Wellesley College* for 1878-1879, mentioned that "fourteen safe and convenient boats have been furnished." But it was not until 1892 that crews were given formal training.[7] Also, both Radcliffe and Barnard Colleges built tennis and basketball courts even before constructing a gymnasium.[8]

Physical educators soon found themselves in a quandary. Student enthusiasm for sport was clearly on the rise while at the same time interest in precision gymnastic drills waned steadily. Writing for the *American Physical Education Review* in 1898, Harriet Ballintine complained that by and large students would only exercise if the work were pleasing and stimulating. Otherwise, they became bored quite easily. The critical task for physical educators, therefore, was to decide which forms of exercise were best fitted to arouse an interest in more students. After reviewing the matter, Ballintine concluded that the growing demand among students for "exercise in which there is an element of play cannot be overlooked."[9] In her opinion, the greatest benefit of sport came from its outdoor orientation. Exercising in the open air and sunlight provided far greater benefits than indoor gymnastics. Students must spend enough time out of doors to "overcome the pernicious effects of a sedentary life." Physical educators, therefore, must make a special effort to assume the direction of organized sports.[10]

Ballintine was not alone in her assessment of sport and gymnastics. Throughout the 1890s, and beyond, physical educators began to reassess their programs. Wellesley gymnastic director Lucille Hill conceded that gymnastics had proven very successful in correcting individual defects and providing antidotes for bad posture and improper clothing. Yet she quickly qualified her support, stating that physical educators used them too much. In doing so, she explained, they failed to obtain the nerve stimulation that came from natural play. If games and sports were organized properly by the director of physical training, then "the gymnastic and corrective value can be gotten out of sport and the fun too." Gymnastics, Hill concluded were artificial exercises, and Americans paid entirely too much attention to the artificial and far too little to the development of a more natural play instinct.[11]

Sports, if used properly, should not completely replace structured gymnastics. Many physical educators believed that sports would instead stimulate interest in all forms of physical training. Such a combined system of gymnastics and sport could flourish if a different definition of gymnastics could be applied. Instead of being the exclusive means to fitness, gymnastics might serve as required conditioning for participation in sports. In that way, a student's physical fitness for sports could be determined in gymnastic classes. Any pupil deemed unfit for the more strenuous forms of exercise would be barred from athletics and thus spared from injury. Those students who were allowed to participate would receive expert instruction in the various sports. In addition, "trained examiners" would closely supervise the contest to further guard the health of the participants. Such an arrangement would be far safer than the haphazard manner in which student sports clubs operated.[12] Through such a program, educators hoped that student interest in gymnasium work could be maintained.[13]

Some experts on the other hand, saw little merit in keeping gymnastic programs. For example, Dr. Thomas Woody of Teacher's College of Columbia University believed strongly that games and sports should entirely replace the various systems of gymnastics still in use. Woody wrote that sports provided greater physical benefits for students. But these benefits went far beyond the mere building of physical vitality. Woody complained that gymnastic training was incomplete. Students who performed movements only upon command of an gymnastics instructor did not develop their bodies and minds adequately. The discipline and control imposed by the instructor, he explained, did not train the student in self-discipline or self-control, or give any opportunity for self-expression as did sports.[14]

Many women's physical educators at women's colleges acted quickly to include sporting activities into their curricula. Most often their chief reason for doing so was the fear that student enthusiasm for established gymnastic drills was rapidly dwindling. In addition to incorporating sports and games into the official program, physical educators sought to formalize hitherto unofficial student sporting activities. They replaced student-run sports clubs, especially in tennis and basketball, with more closely supervised athletic association. This supervision was most commonly provided by a board composed of students and headed by a faculty advisor, usually the college physician or physical education director.[15] By so doing, sports could be transformed from mere student recreation. In the words of Hill, it could be "raised to the dignity of an important branch of education."[16]

The adoption of sporting activities solved many long-standing problems, not the least of which was student antipathy towards traditional gymnastic drill. Outdoor games also did more than anything else to alleviate the chronic lack of indoor space experienced by so many small women's colleges.[17] Additionally, gymnasium work had always been plagued by the perceived dangers of breathing respired air. Such was clearly not a problem with outdoor sports such as tennis or golf. Many authorities also favored these sports because they believed them to be more time-efficient. Ballintine, for instance, described basketball as the ideal form of physical training. It provided more exercise in less time than gymnastics. For the average college woman with limited time for exercise, this one feature of sport alone was of paramount importance.[18]

To silence critics further, experts filled volumes with statistics proving that sports obtained the same results as gymnastics.[19] Finally, many authorities cited the supposed development of social values as reason enough for their inclusion of sports into the official curriculum. Debates over the place of sports in women's physical education would continue for many more years as physical educators incorporated sports and games into their programs while at the same time searching diligently for a way to assert control over them.

Physical educators had tried to organize carefully supervised programs of exercise, backed up by meticulous anthropometric examinations never doubting that the outcome would be a stronger student population. Competitive athletics, however, changed the terms of the debate. The rapid adoption of sports raised many question for which most college physical educators had no ready answers. Many authorities, while believing that recreational sports contributed greatly to health, feared that intense competition could damage the physical and emotional well-being of their students. As sports grew, school leaders would have to re-examine their goals and priorities. Lucille Hill wrote that she foresaw many "warm debates over exactly *how much* and *how keen* competition is desirable to attain the true object of athletics."[20] Many physical educators wondered if athletics would promote extreme competitiveness and muscularity while eroding grace and refinement.[21] Much of the next three decades would be spent analyzing the relationship between womanhood, femininity, and athleticism.[22]

Physical educators had been successful to the extent that few critics still believed that college women could not endure the rigors of higher education. Advocates further claimed that even beyond the domain of the college classroom, the legacy of sports was of great benefit to women. Writing for *Good Housekeeping* in 1902, Alice Fallows praised basketball as a builder of vigorous health. Women who played the sport not only improved their physical strength and endurance, but also developed "well-behaved, obedient nervous systems." The self-control and quick judgement developed by the game were well "worth the price of many strenuous half-hours" spent playing the game. Basketball imparted a life-long legacy of health and served as an unequalled cure for the ill-health of women. It should be cherished, the author concluded, by American women who too often lapsed into the miseries of nervous prostration.[23]

Many popular magazines celebrated the new standard of feminine health. *Good Housekeeping* especially filled its pages with tributes to "the girls of today." The magazine decreed that a remarkable turnaround had taken place in women's health. It noted, for example, that fainting (once quite the fashion among Victorian women) had become an "outgrown ideal." "Today's girl" would consider such behavior a disgrace. Young women who once took pride in poor health had found new sources of health hardly dreamed of by earlier generations. Now, girls "boasted of their muscles and how they could play golf all day or skate half the night without turning a hair."[24]

Other magazines concurred in this reappraisal. A *Ladies' Home Journal* editorial claimed that sports had forever vanquished the swooning damsel of an earlier time. The magazine happily reported that people no longer equated weakness with social position or feminine charm. As one *Woman's Home Companion* author stated, the pale, shrinking girl of the drawing room was no longer believed to be endowed with all sorts of heavenly attributes. Now, she was simply suspected of having a bad liver.[25]

In a 1903 *Good Housekeeping* article, Charles Loomis suggested that if any American girl needed a role model, she should look to California. On average, the West Coast girl grew up to be taller, heavier, stronger, and prettier than the Eastern girl. The reason for this superiority was readily apparent to Loomis. The warm climate enabled the California girl to ride, swim, walk, or golf all year in clean, fresh air. These activities led to greater health which in turn produced greater beauty.[26]

Improved fitness became such a popular subject that many magazines began publishing regular health advice columns advocating exercise for girls. Beginning in 1902, for example, *Ladies' Home Journal* started just such a series. Columns such as "Good Health for Girls," "Pretty Girl Questions," and "A Five Minute Daily Exercise" were regular features of the magazine for that decade. The earliest column championed the latest fad of New York girls: the punching bag. Benefits of its daily use included grace, poise, a springing step, improved complexion, and a cure for dyspepsia.[27] Over the next years, these articles (most of them written by Emma Walker, M.D.) praised exercise in general and vigorous outdoor games specifically. Girls were encouraged to take up golf, rowing, swimming, and tennis on a regular basis. Walker urged her girl readers not to let a day pass without indulging in some form of exercise that caused "a general perspiration of the whole body."[28]

All girls, the magazine noted, should exercise regularly, not just those who were naturally athletic. In her "Girl Problems" column of April, 1902, Margaret Sangster answered a letter from a girl with an "inherited weakness of the lungs." The girl had written complaining that she would very much like to try the new physical culture exercises but her parents, believing them to be too strenuous, suggested that she take up needle-point instead. Sangster replied that despite advice to the contrary, the girl should "drop the idea of needle-craft completely. You need fresh air, plenty of exercise and an object that will keep you out-of-doors."[29]

As the twentieth century began, exercise had certainly gained a measure of legitimacy in women's health. With the introduction of sports and games, the nature of exercise had also changed. What was very slow to change, however, were the assumptions about the role of women in society. A strong undercurrent of very conservative thinking ran through a great deal of pro-fitness arguments. At a time in which many Americans nervously discussed the dangers of declining birth rates, heavy European immigration, eugenics, and even race suicide, the image of a stronger woman was indeed very appealing to some observers.

Many champions of increased fitness for women believed that exercise would enable them to perform their traditional roles. Writing for *Ladies' Home Journal*, Mary Mullet praised collegiate physical education programs for making women bigger and stronger. Yet she quickly noted that this new-found strength would not produce a different woman, merely a better one. Simply because her health had improved did not mean that she would seek to change her natural role. College graduates would still marry and do housework. The only difference was that many women, through their earlier physical training, had escaped the invalidism that had once so thoroughly plagued women. The newer, better woman would be "perfectly able to toy with a broom and amply able to knead the daily bread."[30] Similarly, Christine Herrick wrote in the *Illustrated Sporting News* that thanks to athletics, outdoor living, and indoor training, the woman of the future would be a much finer creature than the weak and nervous woman hitherto known. She concluded that the strength and poise derived from athletics would enable a young woman to fulfill her "obvious destiny" and become a successful wife and mother.[31]

Another related argument reinforced the conservative nature of much pro-fitness rhetoric. Even strong defenders of exercise believed that athletics belonged only to the young. Anne O'Hagan wrote that physical training would undoubtedly be unnecessary for the adult woman. The safeguards against the mental strain of study would not be needed after graduation. Moreover, she continued, once a woman attained full growth and development, exercise did not have the same effect as it did on younger girls.[32]

Implicit in this reasoning was the belief that exercise in youth bestowed a life-long legacy of health. The woman who had been rescued from ill-health and strengthened by sports should, after her youth, content herself with the traditional roles of wife and mother. As yet, there did not exist a widespread belief that the adult woman would either need or want to continue her sporting activities or daily exercises. Many changes would have to occur to prepare the way for the emergence of a true sportswoman.

Chapter Four Notes

1. Dorothy S. Ainsworth, *The History of Physical Education in Colleges for Women, As Illustrated by Barnard, Bryn Mawr, Elmira, Goucher, Mills, Mount Holyoke, Radcliffe, Rockford, Smith, Vassar, Wellesley, and Wells* (New York: A.S. Barnes, 1930), pp. 35, 38.

2. Burton J. Bledstein, *The Culture of Professionalism. The Middle-Class and the Development of Higher Education* (New York: W.W. Norton, 1976), pp. 39, 90. See also, Robert Wiebe, *The Search for Order, 1877-1920* (New York: Hill and Wang, 1967).

3. Ainsworth, *The History of Physical Education*, p. 49.

4. Persis Harlow McCurdy, "The History of Physical Training at Mount Holyoke College," *American Physical Education Review (March 1909), pp. 146-147.*

5. Sophia Foster Richardson, "Tendencies in Athletics for Women in Colleges and Universities," *Popular Science* (February 1897), pp. 517-518.

6. Ainsworth, *The History of Physical Education*, 29, 72. Ainsworth also lists the following information:

College	Pool Opened	Swimming Required
Bryn Mawr	1895	1908
Wells	1911	1913
Goucher	1888	1915
Vassar	1889	1917
Radcliffe	1900	1920
Mills	1924	1926
Rockford	1921	1925

7. *Calendar of Wellesley College, 1878-1879*, p. 63. See also, Ainsworth, *The History of Physical Education*, p. 29.

8. *Catalog of Barnard College, 1917-1918*, p. 76. Radcliffe's gymnasium was built on the site of the tennis and basketball courts in 1898. New fields were then constructed, see *Report of Radcliffe College, 1884-1903*, p. 27.

9. Harriet Isabel Ballintine, "Out-of-Door Sports for College Women," *American Physical Education Review* (March 1898), p. 38.

10. *Ibid.*, p. 29.

11. Cited in Richardson, "Tendencies in Athletics," *Popular Science* (February 1897), p. 519.

68

12. Lucille Eaton Hill, "The New Athletics," *Wellesley College News* (October 29, 1902), p. 1.

13. Richardson, "Tendencies in Athletics," *Popular Science* (February 1897), p. 520. See also, Ballintine, "Out-of-Door Sports," *American Physical Education Review* (March 1898), pp. 39-40.

14. Cited in Ainsworth, *The History of Physical Education*, pp. 10-11.

15. *Ibid.*, p. 79. According to Ainsworth, most college athletic associations were formed during the 1890s. She lists the following dates of association founding: Bryn Mawr, 1891; Smith, 1893; Radcliffe and Vassar, 1895; Mount Holyoke, Goucher, and Wellesley, 1896; Barnard, 1897. While most associations were headed by the P.E. Department, the college physician assumed that role both at Mount Holyoke and Goucher.

16. Hill, "The New Athletics," *Wellesley College News* (October 29, 1902), p. 1.

17. Martha H. Verbrugge, *Able-Bodied Womanhood. Personal Hygiene and Social Change in Nineteenth-Century Boston* (New York: Oxford University Press, 1988), p. 39.

18. Ballintine, "Out-of-Door Sports," *American Physical Education Review* (March 1898), p. 39.

19. Betty Spears, "The Emergence of Women in Sport," in Barbara J. Hoepner, ed., *Women's Athletics: Coping with Controversy* (Washington, D.C.: AAHPER Publications, 1974), p. 33.

20. Hill, "The New Athletics," *Wellesley College News* (October 29, 1902), p. 1.

21. Verbrugge, *Able-Bodied Womanhood*, p. 158.

22. The position of collegiate physical educators on the subject of competitive athletics for women is covered in greater detail in Chapter Six of this work.

23. Alice Katherine Fallows, "Basket Ball: A Builder-Up of Vigorous Women," *Good Housekeeping* (March 1902), pp. 198-200.

24. "The Thoughtful Hour," *Good Housekeeping* (August 1899), pp. 92-93; See also, Dorothy Dix, "The Girl of Today," *Good Housekeeping* (March 1916), p. 289; Peter Clark Macfarlane, "Schools of Fun and Fellowship," *Good Housekeeping* (May 1914), p. 587.

25. "Editorial Page," *Ladies' Home Journal* (August 1916), p. 10; J. Nilsen Laurvik, "The American Girl Out-of-Doors," *Woman's Home Companion* (August 1912), p. 17.

26. Charles Loomis, "The California Girl," *Ladies' Home Journal* (October 1903), p. 290.

27. Emma Walker, M.D., "Good Health for Girls," *Ladies' Home Journal* (March 1902), p. 33.

28. Emma Walker, M.D., "Good Health for Girls," *Ladies' Home Journal* (June 1902), p. 31.

29. Margaret Sangster, "Girl Problems," *Ladies' Home Journal* (April 1902), p. 33.

30. Mary Mullet, "A Swarm of Twelve Hundred Girls," *Ladies' Home Journal* (June 1906), p. 5.

31. Catherine Terhune Herrick, "Schoolgirl Athletes in Track and Field," *The Illustrated Sporting News* (June 6, 1903), p. 15.

32. Anne O'Hagan, "The Athletic Girl," *Munsey's Magazine* (August 1901), p. 734.

CHAPTER FIVE

Redefining Beauty: Marketing the Sportswoman

As the nineteenth century drew to a close, the sportswoman, in the strictest sense, had not yet truly emerged. Despite the attention given by historians to exercise and sports programs in women's colleges, evidence suggests that women in general were rather ambivalent about the subject. There was as yet very little thought that exercise or sport would be necessary or even useful for women beyond college age. Writing for *Outing*, John Habberton noted that American women beyond college age were simply not encouraged to exercise. The much-heralded gymnasium could not be found outside the ivied walls of women's colleges. Given these circumstances, there were few mature women who "deliberately and systematically" took some form of exercise.[1]

One important factor in shaping the nature and level of interest in sports and exercise for women involved the prevailing standards of beauty. Reinforced by common medical thought, fashion, and dietary customs, the plump, non-athletic look served as the dominant standard of beauty for quite a long time. Many changes on various social levels would have to transpire before the acceptance of the athletic look displaced the older standard. Not until the second decade of the twentieth century would the sportswoman emerge as a powerful, if not dominant cultural symbol.

For many decades, both the prevailing models of health and fashion promoted ideals that were anything but athletic. Popular medical theorists held that fat promoted health. Health experts regarded plumpness as a clear sign of well-being, especially for women. Rather than turning out diet or exercise books, doctors and faddists alike produced works such as the 1878 work, *How to Be Plump*. Its author, Dr. Thomas Duncan, urged his readers, especially women, to eat starchy foods, fats, and sweets in order to achieve what he termed "florid plumpness."[2] Instead of prescribing exercise for their adult female patients, many physicians instead favored "The Rest Cure." Under this regimen, patients were confined to bed and encouraged to eat at frequent intervals. Famed neurologist, S. Weir Mitchell, carried this practice to extremes, forbidding his resting female patients any movement. They were forbidden to talk or use their hands, and were fed and washed by others. If they wished to move, a maid or nurse was summoned to assist so the patient would not have to exert any energy.[3] On average, this treatment lasted six to eight weeks, and weight gains of fifty pounds or more were not uncommon.[4]

Contemporary fashion did its part to complement medical thinking. Fashionable dress for women at this time clearly emphasized (some would say distorted) a very ample bust and posterior creating what historian Lois Banner has labeled the voluptuous woman.[5] By far, the most celebrated example of the voluptuous woman was famed actress Lillian Russell. As one fan wrote of her, "there was plenty of her to see, and we liked that," she was beautiful, stately, broad and ample.[6] The *New York World* praised Russell's figure as being "royally gowned with all the undulations of a prima donna's figure molded graciously in ripples of motion." For decades, Russell endured as the most famous beauty and most photographed woman in America. She stood as voluptuousness incarnate, and brought great elegance to the ideal.[7]

Russell achieved fame not only for her stage performances but also for her appearances at the Waldorf Hotel dining room. There she regularly displayed her legendary appetite.[8] On one rather infamous occasion, she and her frequent dinner companion "Diamond" Jim Brady held an informal contest to determine who could eat the most in one sitting. Russell prevailed although the situation compelled her to remove her corset.[9]

One of the earliest and most successful challenges to the voluptuous standard came in the form of celebrated British actress, Lily Langtry. In 1882, the actress embarked upon an American theater tour, playing upon her reputation as mistress of the Prince of Wales and other rumored scandals carefully and deliberately placed. Her first reception in America was not, however, overwhelming. Many critics believed that her height and muscular body were grave liabilities on the American stage. In 1882, for example, *Music and Drama* wrote that early exercise had eliminated roundness from Langtry's figure. Such was a fatal flaw, because as the magazine noted, the American public desired "roundness of figure."[10]

Langtry was in fact tall (5'8") and her figure did indeed reflect years of exercise beginning in childhood. She had, moreover, carried into adulthood the habit of daily exercise. Langtry was not shy about her preference for exercise and responded to her early detractors by touting the merits of long early morning walks.[11] Within a few years, she had triumphed over most of her critics and had won acceptance for her athletic appearance. *Cosmopolitan* magazine declared in 1899 that Langtry was now the most famous professional beauty in the world. Far from attacking her trim form, the magazine proclaimed that "her noted loveliness" was the result of her simple, wholesome, and vigorous early life. It was, "the product of the cream and brown bread, the peaches and sunshine of the island where she was born and where she ran about a wild tomboy girl."[12]

In its beauty, theater, and society features, *Cosmopolitan* presented to its readers other examples of this new beauty ideal. The Empress of Austria, for example, had been famous for her beauty for several decades. Much as did the younger Langtry, the Empress had been the beneficiary of a vigorous childhood, living in the mountains, dressed in coarse cloth and wool, and frolicking as "a madcap tomboy." She remained a celebrated beauty, the magazine claimed, "despite being fifty-two years of age."[13] *Cosmopolitan* singled out others among the European nobility for praise, such as the "dazzlingly fair" Lady Londonderry of England. In appearance she was worlds removed from Russell, being described as "tall as a daughter of the gods, slim as the legendary alder from which Odin made women."[14]

Not only were beauty standards changing on the European stage but also among the artistic community. The nude, once made famous by artists such as Bouguereau had been revived but also significantly changed. The models so prominent in the 1870s, those with "robust frames and abundant flesh" were no longer popular. In their places now stood smaller, thinner, even spare women "whose contours never awaken memories of the antique."[15]

Such descriptions of foreign nobility, beautiful actresses, and slender models lent great appeal to the new athletic look. It would not, however, remain foreign for long as American women of rank, class, and stage began to adopt it. In the numerous beauty columns in popular magazines, American women that were singled out as the most beautiful or most successful upon the stage were described as tall, graceful, svelte, and exquisitely slim.[16]

In the seemingly innumerable analyses of beautiful women, the popular press of the day repeated the same advice. Beautiful women (whether actresses, nobility, or socialites) attained their beauty by living right, eating right, and exercising.[17] As the twentieth century neared, the ideal of the voluptuous woman was losing favor. In 1898, *Cosmopolitan* announced that "stout women are never fascinating." The fascinating woman "may be tall or small, but she must be slender, graceful, lithe, and willowy."[18]

Fashion and beauty features of popular magazines bore witness to changes that would introduce the athletic look to a broader audience. In a similar way, the society news columns of the same magazines continued this development. In particular, the attention given to the elite summer resort communities proved very influential in shaping the image of the sportswoman. In the late nineteenth century and into the twentieth, it was customary for the nation's socially prominent families to spend the summer months at seaside resorts thereby escaping the city, along with its crowds and heat.[19]

At the pinnacle of summer resort living stood the town of Newport, Rhode Island. Popular magazines reported at length on the lifestyle there, highlighting the lavish parties, the expensive cottages, and the staffs of servants. Nowhere in the United States, reported *Cosmopolitan*, was luxurious living so impressively displayed as in Newport.[20] The magazine proclaimed it the most expensive city in America. As testament to this status, it informed its readers that the average Newport cottage rented for three to seven thousand dollars for the typical June through September lease period. Adding the cost of maintaining the proper number of servants, hosting the socially acceptable number of parties, and wearing the required formal attire, *Cosmopolitan* calculated that a Newport socialite could not make ends meet on one thousand dollars per day.[21] One common anecdote told of a newspaper reporter who remarked that the Newport summer colony seemed to devote itself to pleasure regardless of expense. He was quickly corrected by locals that in fact Newportites devoted themselves to expense regardless of pleasure.[22]

Much of Newport society revolved around the famed Newport Casino. Although serving many purposes, the Casino served first and foremost as a tennis club with the finest courts in the nation.[23] Tennis enjoyed great popularity in Newport with "tennis week" being the climax of the summer season. At first, the annual tennis tournament held during this week was contested among the summer inhabitants. When the United States Lawn Tennis Association formed in 1881, "tennis week" was transformed into a national championship tournament with entrants drawn from other clubs across the country.[24]

In addition to providing competition for refined gentlemen, sports such as tennis also served as opportunity for respectable social encounters, giving men and women something fashionable to do together. Yet women's participation in sports at this time proved to be quite different from that of their male companions. The slow entrance of women into the sporting world was especially evident at Newport. Well into the 1870s, efforts by mature women to strengthen the body were still considered vulgar and beneath the aristocratic standards of the resort. While men made polo, squash, and tennis synonymous with Newport, women's daily activity seemed largely limited to being driven to the Casino in coaches during the day and hosting lavish parties in the evening.[25]

As the 1880s opened, some women did take up croquet and tennis, but only as a part of courtship. Accordingly, they wore their regular confining dress, including their corsets. Marie Wagner (national women's tennis champion of 1906) remembered that in her youth, no woman would set foot on a tennis court unless "upholstered with a corset, a starched piqué skirt heavily button trimmed, starched shirtwaist with long sleeves and cuff links, a high collar and a four-in-hand necktie."[26] Furthermore, the pace of play was not brisk, as sweating was not considered genteel at anytime, least of all while courting.[27]

In addition to being part of the courtship ritual, sports also became an occasional medical prescription. Much as college physical educators designed calisthenics for coeds, so too did some summer resort physicians prescribe sports such as tennis or croquet for their women patients. Unlike college students, however, women of Newport's summer colony generally lacked competitive zest. As described by one observer, Mrs. Rita Lydig played tennis at the Newport Casino once in a great while upon the advice of her physician. At least she would hit a few aimless balls across the net in the general direction of the patient professional. She always wore her regular confining dress, heavy gloves, and "a veil of impenetrable thickness" which covered her entire face, except for her eyes.[28]

By the end of the 1880s, tennis had begun to change. At the annual men's championship tournament at Newport (which moved in 1915 to Forest Hills, New York) a more vigorous game with hard strokes and rushing the net became the norm. Also, gentlemen began to abandon their formal attire in search of the freedom of movement required by the new game.[29] Some women could also be found playing the faster-paced game and wearing less restrictive clothing. Women playing tennis strictly for its own sake were apparently novel. In fact, in 1893 when socialite Ava Willing Astor played a vigorous tennis match (wearing bloomers) it created quite a stir. So arresting was the sight that *Vogue* devoted special coverage to the spectacle. The magazine referred to Astor and friends as "the Moderns" thus lending much publicity to sports for women.[30]

Such elite communities, although small in number, were of critical importance in shaping the image of sports for both men and women. The society news reported from such resorts as Newport created the lasting impression that sports such as tennis or golf were essentially activities of the upper class who possessed the leisure time to play and the finances to join clubs. This link with expensive clubs lent to sports what one writer referred to as a distinctly "social tone of the highest class, for only people of the best position are in any way concerned with the best clubs."[31] With such prominent women as the Astors playing the game, it was easy for society writers to label tennis as "quite the thing" for women.[32]

Early competitive sports for women benefitted greatly from this air of exclusivity. Tournaments were carefully controlled so that only those of "assured social position" were permitted to enter. The Ladies' National Championship, for example, was conducted by invitation only. As a result, all of the finest lady tennis players also belonged to the "best families," making such tournaments "the most brilliant and fashionable affairs of the Season."[33]

The appeal of the country club was great. In a short time, golf and tennis had risen from the status of marginal activities for women to very exclusive and fashionable pursuits. These clubs were, as *Collier's* described in 1900, "centers of wealth and solid respectability" and no important town should be without one, "as lavish as funds could provide."[34] Luxurious clubs soon sprang up across the country. For example, the Woman's Athletic Club of Chicago boasted of a $100,000 club house, pool, gymnasium, and indoor track as well as the traditional golf and tennis facilities. Such accommodations did not come cheaply as attested to by the one hundred dollar membership fee.[35] Rivaling this club, the Berkeley Ladies' Athletic Club stood as New York's most fashionable and exclusive club. As one writer of the *Fortnightly Review* described, there were none like it in "completeness and perfection of equipment, luxury of surroundings, and exclusiveness in its membership. It is quite the thing to belong to the Berkeley." It was not an easy feat either, even if one could afford the seventy-five dollar initiation fee and the forty dollar annual dues.[36]

Sports had become a necessary activity for anyone wishing to gain entry to polite and refined society. As *Cosmopolitan* proclaimed, anyone, "if they wish to be numbered among the smart set of England and America, must be adept at all kinds of outdoor sports."[37] Actually, not all outdoor sports were included in that statement: only the status club-style sports such as golf or tennis. Tennis especially, noted one prominent physical education author, had attained distinction in the public eye, numbering among its adherents many noted citizens of the world, as well as finding great favor among the reigning families of Europe.[38] The appeal of country club sports had great effects on other sports. In 1896, *Cosmopolitan* reported that reliable rumors indicated that in England, France, and America, those of the bluest blood had abandoned cycling in favor of tennis and as a result of their example, cycling had fallen into general disfavor.[39]

Another writer took exception to this statement and in 1899 corrected it by proclaiming that the upper class had never actually given its stamp of approval to the wheel and it was essentially popular only among "the middle-class of small tradesmen, clerks, and mechanics."[40] Regardless of who had taken up the sport, *Collier's* announced in 1901 that cycling in general did not enjoy its former popularity. Since the 1890s, the magazine noted, other sports most notably golf had claimed a greater share of attention and support. By explanation, *Collier's* remarked that golf had a great advantage over other sports by being a more dignified pastime.[41]

A popular health movement, emerging late in the century further nurtured the developing athletic look for women. Author and showman Bernarr Macfadden served as the movement's most vocal proponent and in 1899 he began publishing the magazine *Physical Culture* which would run for the next half-century. Macfadden's message was a mixture of old health advice combined with a more strident advocacy of exercise and a very explicit emphasis upon beauty. Targeting the middle-class, Macfadden's movement introduced the concept of the sportswoman to an even broader audience.

There was indeed much in Macfadden's message that was many decades old. The early nineteenth century notion of positive and negative health, for example, was carried over by Macfadden who reminded his readers that simply avoiding sickness did not constitute health. Unless people enjoyed perfect health they stood perilously near illness. Exercise could both replenish and preserve vital power, thereby safeguarding the body against disease. Macfadden believed that most illnesses struck because of weaknesses in the chest and abdominal muscles. As did health writers five decades before him, he proclaimed that the first step in treating sickness was to increase vital power by strengthening the muscles of the chest and stomach.[42] Early nineteenth century physicians stimulated the stomach and intestines with drugs; Macfadden substituted exercise. Early health reformers urged people to expand their chests by walking or running; Macfadden prescribed isometrics.

As did the Thompsonians, homeopaths, and phrenologists before him, Macfadden proclaimed his movement to be democratic. Exercise, he complained, had been too closely tied to bastions of privilege such as the college gymnasium. Such facilities did give certain men or women a decided advantage.

But, wrote Macfadden disciple Jonathan Treloar in 1904, it would be a mistake to suppose that simply because people had no such access that they were shut out from the benefits of exercise. Abraham Lincoln, Treloar reminded his readers, made himself a scholar without attending college. Similarly then, many men and women could accomplish the work of repairing their own health by persistent exercise in their own rooms. Such programs as espoused by Macfadden did not necessitate expensive or hard-to-find apparatus.[43]

Macfadden wanted to convince his readers that above all else, his physical culture program was for everyone. Exercise was not the sole province of the prize fighter, weight lifter, or those who desired only to secure some phenomenal or abnormal physical development. It was not just for the athlete, but for the everyday man or woman who wished to get everything out of life that nature intended. Exercise would produce not just strength but also health, vigor, suppleness, and above all beauty.[44]

Macfadden's bold emphasis on beauty set him apart from his predecessors. For Macfadden followers, health or mere physical efficiency should not be the only reward of an exercise program. "There should be," one writer added, "an artistic consideration." In taking up exercise, not the least important objective ought to be "beauty, which distinguishes the perfectly developed man or woman."[45] Macfadden made the link between exercise and beauty (especially for women) the cornerstone of his message. It was a fact, he wrote in *Cosmopolitan*, that "high health" in women means in seventy-five percent of all cases good looks, if not indeed true beauty. Exercise would prove invaluable for women for enhancing personal charm and especially for increasing "beauty of form."[46] This beauty of form, according to Macfadden was the key part of "the great feminine desideratum." It was attained only by physical culture, because there could be no real beauty without strength.[47]

Macfadden, it has been argued by historians, was a "worshipper of the bosom." He was convinced that well-formed breasts were evidence of a woman's muscular health, sexual attractiveness, and reproductive fitness. Writing that "superb womanhood is indicated by a good bust," he offered exercises for their improvement, going as far as publishing a series of photographs of bare-breasted women exercising.[48] Indicative of Macfadden's opinion, he presented his readers with the example of actress Maude O'Dell. After only a brief time spent in physical training, she now possessed what Macfadden believed to be the "perfect form." *Physical Culture* listed her measurements as 42-25-39. O'Dell stated that she was very grateful to the science of physical culture for re-sculpting both her figure and her purse. Her stage appearances were now netting her a very handsome sum annually.[49]

Macfadden focused on women's "sexual fitness" for a number of reasons. A skilled promoter and showman, he realized that in an era in which older Victorian attitudes toward sexuality were unraveling, sex appeal sold magazines. In a similar vein, Macfadden changed careers in the 1920s. Eventually he left *Physical Culture* and went instead into the business of publishing detective and romance magazines, finding apparently that sex and violence sold better than sex and muscles.[50]

In addition, Macfadden was obsessed with the idea of breeding a vigorous new generation, so much so that his ex-wife referred to him as the Great Begatsby. He believed (as did many in decades before him) that a woman's sexual vitality was doubly precious for it defined not only her health but that of a future race as well.[51] Macfadden and others clearly embraced the early nineteenth century theory that women exerted greater influence than men over heredity. This theory lingered into the twentieth century as illustrated by a 1905 *Popular Science* article. Its author, Dr. Lapthorn Smith, repeated the old axiom that if women were not healthy, men could not be good fathers, "for the simple reason that the men contribute so little toward the new being."[52]

Macfadden offered a two-fold message. Exercise built vitality (especially reproductive fitness) and enhanced beauty. Of these two, the link between the athletic look and beauty would become the most powerful. The pressure to conform to the new standard of beauty was likewise strong. As testimony to this ongoing trend, Lillian Russell began a career of dieting in the late nineties, especially after an 1896 stage review compared her to a white elephant. For the next decade her diets gained as much publicity as her stage performances.[53]

As older Victorian standards of prudery began to crumble, the message of athletic beauty became more explicit and powerful. As expounded upon by Macfadden and his disciples, athleticism would not only be equated with beauty and reproductive fitness but also with sexual attractiveness. The chief advocate of this line of thought was Australian swimmer and showperson Annette Kellerman. In many respects Kellerman's approach was similar to that of the mid-nineteenth century health reformers who had overcome personal weakness and then offered themselves as proof that a particular regimen did indeed work. Kellerman had been a weak child who could not walk without the support of heavy steel braces on her legs. Yet through exercise (in this case swimming), she not only escaped invalidism but became a champion swimmer and the star attraction of many American water shows. During the 1910s and 1920s, she wrote books and pamphlets and toured the nation offering herself as "an example of full bodily development approximating the Ideal Ratio of Femininity."[54]

What distinguished Kellerman from such nineteenth century health advocates as Sylvester Graham or John Harvey Kellogg was her very explicit message to women on the importance of beauty. Kellerman complained of a double standard. For centuries, she noted, people had recognized that men should have a sound mind in a healthy body. But if a woman tried to cultivate her body, she was accused of "trying to exert her charms to no good end." This was because feminine "beauty of body" had long been held as a thing of doubtful value because it was so closely associated with sexual attraction. A woman trying to increase the beauty of her figure was immediately suspect. A married women was especially limited, for if she tried to keep her figure after marriage she was accused of seeking further loves.[55]

Kellerman proclaimed that the time was long overdue for a new gospel of feminine beauty. Simply put, it was a woman's right and duty to be beautiful. It also followed that the best means of achieving this beauty was through muscular development and diet.[56] Beauty was of such paramount importance because happiness (both immediate and future) depended on it. Grave consequences were at stake because a woman who failed to develop beauty of body would fail in finding love. Kellerman's advice to married women proved even more explicit. Not only must a woman develop beauty of body, but she must keep it as well. As Kellerman sadly pointed out, the world was full of unhappy homes from which love had flown with the passing of the lithe figure of girlhood. The chief reason for this unfortunate circumstance was the popular fallacy that marriage blinded a man forever to feminine charm and eliminated the necessity of the wife's remaining attractive. To the contrary, Kellerman adamantly maintained that "man's love must have feminine beauty as a flower must have water."[57]

To prove her point, she pointed to the nation's divorce statistics. According to her, at least seventy-five percent of all divorces granted on the grounds of unfaithfulness or desertion actually occurred because the wife had lost her physical charm. If a married woman faded at age thirty and grew fat at age forty, no "system of morals" could save the marriage. Only beauty, she concluded, could light the fires of love and keep them burning: not warmed slippers or attractive dishes made from leftovers.[58]

By linking beauty with athleticism, writers such as Macfadden and Kellerman gave the athletic look for women powerful appeal, signalling the ultimate downfall of the voluptuous standard. By 1900, Lily Langtry was the undisputed queen of beauty and writers forgot their earlier dislike of her classic features and athletic frame.[59] Instead of advocating plumpness, writers now inveighed against it. *Collier's* magazine, for example, in 1901 published an article entitled "The Perils of Obesity." The magazine warned its readers that fat blocked the whole machinery of the body. It clogged the muscles and weakened the heart. Women especially, the magazine noted, should be careful not to allow their muscles to shrink because this allowed fat to gather in folds about the waist and hips which could subsequently shorten the life-span.[60]

In a similar vein, *Cosmopolitan* published a 1910 article written by noted muckraking journalist, Upton Sinclair, warning of the dangers of eating too much. Sinclair wrote that he had long suffered from fatigue and mental and physical exhaustion. He took a year away from his writing and concentrated on his health, living in the open air and taking vigorous exercise. Still, he was not freed from his ills until he incorporated fasting into his program. The success of his fasts (some as long as eleven days) led him to believe that the secret of health could be found in adjusting the quantity of food to the body's exact needs. Sinclair's wife, he reported, had always been frail. But after following his fasting program, she began walking four miles each day and had become a picture of radiant health. She was also engaged in "accumulating muscle with enthusiasm."[61]

Along with this changing attitude toward fat, the athletic look also brought about a very important change in the attitude concerning a woman's age. No longer was thirty or forty years of age viewed as old. Now, all women were encouraged to look as young as they wanted. Writing for *Cosmopolitan* in 1903, one author singled out one thing about the good old days "for which the modern woman never sighed." She referred specifically to the rigid line which marked the boundary between youth and old age. She noted that forty years ago, many women now celebrated for their charm, beauty, and intellect would have relegated to the confining ranks of the dowagers and grandmothers. Women of her time were, she estimated, twenty or thirty years younger that their grandmothers at the same age. The reason for this transformation was quite simple. Women had decided not to grow old and sought means of preserving a youthful appearance. As a means to that end, women should shun the rocking chair and seek recreation in the open air.[62]

Good Housekeeping also endorsed the preservation of youthful appearance. In a 1906 article entitled "Growing Young Again," the magazine presented its readers with a case history of a typical woman. At forty years of age, she had lost her "trim, fine figure." At fifty, she looked really old, and at sixty she was fat, pudgy, and misshapen. But, at sixty-five she began to look into physical culture, and being "a woman of good mind," was not long in discovering the errors of her way. She learned that for thirty years at least, she had been eating vastly too much and exercising too little. Thus enlightened, she became a devotee of physical culture, gave up coffee, and began dieting. Now, at age seventy-five she was once more trim in form and walked with an elastic step with clear eyes and an alert mind.[63]

In advocating exercise, *Good Housekeeping* chose to promote housework as the best exercise for women. In a 1901 article, the magazine praised housework as an invaluable aid to health. It was especially excellent for developing the legs, hips, and ankles. The magazine also urged its readers to "make housekeeping hygienic" by donning loose clothing (without corsets) and shorter skirts for ease of movement and safety.[64] In a 1907 article entitled "Kitchen Gymnastics," *Good Housekeeping* presented its readers with the example of a wealthy woman who complained to her physician of many chronic ills. The doctor replied, "Madam, you are not ill, but suffering from too much help in the kitchen. Dismiss one of your maids and try housework yourself for two or three months." At the end of the second month she reported to her physician that no prescription he had ever given had helped her so much.[65]

According to the article's author, such a prescription for health needed to be given more frequently. He claimed that housework ("woman's natural gymnastics") had changed many a semi-invalid into a healthy woman. It was unfortunate that more women did not do their own housework. It seemed odd, the author puzzled, that the same "woman who thinks it degrading to poke up a pillow, punches an expensive striking bag and fancies her ladyhood less impaired."[66]

Noting the popularity of the topic, *Ladies' Home Journal* hastened to add its opinion on sport and exercise for women. In 1909, the editor admitted that he was somewhat puzzled by the prevailing "curious idea" that good health could be achieved by muscular gymnastics or physical culture. Yet, hundreds of women had written the magazine asking, "give us a physical culture series that we may be healthy."[67]

The magazine was quick to respond but its message was far from original and was in fact quite conservative. In that same 1909 issue, the magazine included an article entitled "Dr. Bentley's Physical Culture for Girls." The article repeated the established belief that once a girl's muscles were developed, strength and vital force were stored for any emergency. Thereafter, a woman needed very little exercise to maintain health.[68]

In 1912, the magazine succeeded in having national fitness authority Dudley Sargent, director of Harvard's Hemenway Gymnasium, write a series. In his first installment Sargent stated that women should not worry about developing the strength and endurance of men. They should instead exercise to secure good carriage, grace, and a good figure which would "inspire admiration in the opposite sex."[69] He recommended exercises such as running, dancing, tennis, and gymnastics because they kept the figure lithe, graceful, and boyish. The boyish figure with "narrow hips, supple body, and slender limbs," was the "ideal figure for women in their early twenties."[70]

These exercises, Sargent prescribed, should be indulged in "from early youth to full maturity." Sargent assumed that once a woman had reached maturity (generally after college) she would give up her "vigorous physical living." Then, her figure would develop into what he termed the Venus type, characterized by a "plump figure, large hips and bust, and fleshy shoulders with beautiful curves and soft lines."[71]

Sargent underscored his position in his second *Ladies' Home Journal* article "Are Athletics Making Girls Masculine?" He stated that qualities developed by athletics such as increased attention, concentration, and self-control were as valuable to women as to men. Yet he still implied that once these qualities were developed by school girls they needed little or no reinforcement later.[72] Although he stated that athletics did not make girls masculine or destroy the beautiful lines and curves of the figure, he suggested that sports be carefully limited or modified to certain "peculiar qualifications" of women. Specifically, he recommended reduced playing time, more rest periods, lighter weights, and especially in the case of basketball, separate rules.[73] Basketball, he believed, placed too great a strain on the heart and lungs. He claimed that he had seen too many breakdowns in tournaments and women's colleges as coeds were driven beyond their physical limits by team loyalty or school pride. He hoped that stricter rules, including the division of the basketball court into three zones (to limit running and jumping) would prevent the players from injuring themselves.[74]

Given Sargent's expressed opinions on the appropriateness of athletics for the grown women, his third *Ladies' Home Journal* article proved quite different. In this article, "After a Woman is 40" (subtitled, "What Form of Exercise is Wise for Her to Take?"), he reversed his position on many points. Two months after writing that the mature woman should abandon athletics and become "plump," he stated that "if a girl learns to play games and participate in athletic sports during youth, there is no reason why she cannot continue to fifty years or more."[75] People, especially women, he noted, allowed themselves to become old from inactivity. Exercise, however, deferred old age and eliminated fat. He urged women to cling to the sports of their youth, adding quickly that these activities should be done only in moderation. Also, overly strenuous sports should be passed over in favor of walking, dancing, croquet, and golf.[76]

In 1912, *Good Housekeeping* carried the article "The Athletic Woman" which further highlighted the importance of athletics for women. Author Anna de Koven agreed that American women abandoned athletic sports and exercise too early in life. These activities produced elasticity of muscles, cheerfulness of spirit, and especially a youthful appearance. De Koven noted that outdoor games not only kept women youthful but were critically important because they led "to mutual interest and comradeship between the sexes." De Koven believed that many American women suffered from loneliness and that "the pursuit of open air exercise with their men-folk" would be a splendid remedy.[77]

This increased emphasis on leisure activities, beauty, and youth were all parts of a larger and more subtle change in the nature of middle-class marriage. The social segregation of the sexes was breaking down as a more companionate marriage became the ideal. The emphasis on youthful appearances, beauty, and male companionship meant that all women (even married women) had to engage in a two-front battle against age and weight.[78] As this message became stronger, readers of popular magazines were confronted with numerous advertisements touting methods for weight loss.

One of the earliest weight loss promoters, the Grecian System of Physical Culture, placed advertisements in *Ladies' Home Journal* as early as 1902. The message of its directors, Prudence and Clarence Barnard of Chicago, would be repeated many times by their mail-order competitors. The Barnards opened by stating that the deepest "heart-secret of every womanly woman" was to retain youth and beauty, or to regain them when lost. After all, they claimed, the middle-aged figure was inexcusable and unnecessary.[79] They promised that the practice of their system would impart those things that every woman wanted, namely "well-rounded arms, pretty neck and shoulders, a full bust, and a good complexion."[80] In closing, they touted their system as the ideal one, equally good for growing girls as well as "those whom time had already touched with the frost of many years." The Barnards would send prospective customers an initial descriptive booklet free of charge.[81]

Annette Kellerman also made great use of the mail-order fitness market. From 1910 through the 1920s, advertisements for her booklet "The Body Beautiful" (available for the price of two cents) could be found in the pages of *Ladies' Home Journal*. In large bold print, accompanied by a photograph of herself attired in tights, she promised readers "*Your* figure can be as Perfect as Mine." She boasted that she had already helped thousands of women become vigorous, healthy, and attractive.[82]

Kellerman's chief rival in mail-order fitness was Susanna Cocroft of Chicago. She urged the readers of *Ladies' Home Journal* to become the women they wished to be. She claimed that 80,000 women were her friends because she had made them well, taught them how to reduce, and had either given them perfect figures, or had helped them retain their youthful form.[83] Cocroft's message was well received. In her autobiography, socialite Nathalie Dana recalled that she was thrilled when she heard that a person in Chicago named Susanna Cocroft would give fitness advice by mail. She wrote immediately and was delighted to learn that by diet and exercise her waistline could be controlled. Dana believed that if she could improve her appearance, she would have a better time at parties.[84]

As was evident in the messages of Kellerman, Cocroft, and others, much of the era's fitness advice centered on ways to increase personal beauty, especially that of the figure. For most writers, beauty was inextricably linked with exercise. Dr. Woods Hutchinson, for example, admonished his *Good*

Housekeeping readers that exercise was the best means of getting and keeping beauty. Beauty, he noted was the "priceless possession which is the right of every woman." To secure it, he suggested that women should "get one good sweat everyday: not a mere glow or perspiration, but a real, genuine, downright, old fashioned, Anglo-Saxon sweat."[85]

Fashion writer Dorothy Cooks offered similar advice to her *Ladies' Home Journal* readers. Fashions, she stated, were for women with "shape." As a result numerous women had written her asking how to develop the bust. Noting that the "woman of superb health" was stimulating and attractive, Cooks urged her readers to take advantage of summer exercises. Specifically, she recommended those exercises that molded "the shoulders and chest and breasts in lovely proportions." According to Cooks, no exercise was better than swimming for firming flabby breasts or correcting flat-chestedness. If they could not swim, Cooks suggested that her readers try tennis or golf as these sports also lifted and rounded a shapeless bosom and hardened flabby arms.[86]

Ladies' Home Journal beauty editor, Louise Paine Benjamin, also noted that nothing worked as well as swimming for women who wished to "improve their chest measure." To reinforce her point, she offered the following poem:

> If you'd acquire a figure trim,
> Lose no time getting in the swim.
> To find the action that she craves,
> The modern girl cuts through the waves.
> She emulates the streamlined trout,
> No hips! They're definitely *out*.
> By swimming strokes her curves are placed,
> Where they belong, above the waist.[87]

Advertising provided the final impetus to the growing popularity of sports and exercise for women. The growth of advertising itself was sudden and dramatic, spurred on by developments during the First World War. Organized as the National War Advisory Board, advertising leaders offered their help to the government. Subsequently, they mounted very impressive campaigns to sell bonds, recruit military personnel, enhance worker morale, and promote food conservation. These advertisements succeeded beyond all expectations, demonstrating that it was quite possible to sway the minds of whole populations and change habits. In addition, under the wartime excess profits taxes, advertising expenses were declared exempt, thereby encouraging experimentation and especially enlarged advertising budgets.[88]

The results of the war-time boom in advertising were spectacular. Historians estimate that the total advertising volume in the United States increased from 682 million dollars in 1914, to 1.4 billion dollars in 1919, to nearly 3 billion dollars in 1929.[89] Encouraged by their war experience, newly emerging national advertisers increased their budgets geometrically. Maxwell House coffee, for example, increased its advertising budget from $19,995 in 1921 to $509,000 in 1927.[90]

Advertisers frequently proclaimed themselves as missionaries of modernity, championing the new against anything which could be considered old-fashioned. This bias ensured that advertising would heavily emphasize those styles or behaviors that were new.[91] In that light, the image of the sportswoman appeared tailor-made. In a *Ladies' Home Journal* advertisement, the Elgin Watch Company hailed its watch as perfect for "the new athletic days." The watch not only kept time but was beautiful and built to "stand the stress of the modern girl's vigorous life."[92] One of the most prominent users of the sportswoman's modern personae were those companies which manufactured hygiene products. The Cellucotton company (later renamed Kotex) spent heavily on an advertising campaign designed to link the use of their product with the modern and elegant classes. Their advertisements praised their customers for being the modern women of the day. These women were active, they travelled, and participated in sports. Not surprisingly, therefore, they were also free of "women's oldest hygienic problem."[93]

Modess, the chief rival of Kotex in the feminine hygiene market, also heavily stressed the modern message. In 1929, Modess ran a multi-part advertising campaign entitled "Modernizing Mother." Each advertisement depicted a mother and daughter engaged in a different sport such as skiing or golf. According to Modess, the modern daughter was "graceful as a greyhound, a star at tennis, golf, riding, or swimming: with not a nerve or ache in her vital body." She had shattered the older myth that it was unladylike to be too healthy. Similarly, she was also smashing other "hide-bound traditions" and hygienic drudgeries which had held her mother in bondage. These fearless modern girls were now teaching their mothers how to escape old-fashioned ideas and be young again.[94]

At first, not all advertisers appreciated the advantage of selling the intangible benefit instead of merely the product. After the war, advertisers more clearly recognized that consumers would rather identify with scenes of higher status than ponder their actual lives. "People are seeking to escape themselves," wrote one contributor to *Advertising and Selling* in 1926, "they want to live in a more exciting world."[95] Accordingly, advertisers sought to give their products a better image by placing them in elegant settings. The central purpose of the advertisement was not to depict reality but rather to sell a product by hinting that the consumer bought not only the product, but also the prestige that went with it.

Advertisers relied on the sportswoman and the elegance of the country club to sell products. Vaseline, for example, ran an advertisement in 1929 in which a woman stated that she had overheard someone saying that Vaseline petroleum jelly was marvelous for weather-beaten skin after golf. What gave this overheard conservation weight was its setting: the locker room of an exclusive country club.[96]

Selling prestige was a prime objective of the early automobile industry. Consequently, the sportswoman appeared with great regularity in automobile advertising as companies hoped to cash in on the appeal of the country club. The 1920 Ford, for example, was pictured parked at a golf course with women golfers in the background. The advertisement noted that people seeing the new Ford parked proudly beside the cool green of the country club would be impressed by its flowing grace of line and contour.[97] Ford's mass-produced cars were hardly luxurious, but Ford hoped that these advertisements would impart just such an appeal. Numerous other automobile manufacturers, including

Cadillac, Buick, Chrysler, Dodge, Overland, and Oldsmobile ran similar advertisements.[98]

Advertising campaigns for Woodbury soap carried the snob appeal of the sportswoman to its greatest extreme. Woodbury advertisements stated that at the country's most fashionable resorts, the most beautiful women were to be seen riding, golfing, swimming, or "making the loveliest pictures as they skate, ski, or toboggan." These same women used Woodbury soap.[99] Generally, Woodbury advertisements specifically mentioned a very prestigious club where all "the fastidious women guests" or "enchantingly pretty debutantes in their new sports frocks from the Riviera" used Woodbury soap to smooth their skin after sports. Mentioned specifically were the Mount Royal in Montreal, the Washington Golf and Country Club, and the Lake Placid Club, unsurpassed, it was claimed, for winter sports.[100]

One of the most dominant (some historians might argue that repressive is a better term) themes in advertising during the 1920s was the constant emphasis on youth. *Ladies' Home Journal*, in a self-promotional advertisement underscored this theme by announcing that its magazine was for "all smart young women, and no woman today need ever grow old." Youth was no longer a simple matter of years, but of spirit, and the spirit of the *Ladies' Home Journal* was youth.[101]

Product advertisements during this decade echoed the beauty advice which demanded that women stay young and attractive. A Palmolive soap advertisement featuring a mother and daughter golfing announced that women should stay young with their daughters by keeping their school-girl complexions. Youth, noted Palmolive, is charm, and youth lost is charm lost. Use of the soap would prevent this loss. The advertisement hinted that Palmolive would enhance more than facial beauty stating that "millions [of women] let it do for their *bodies* what it does for their faces."[102]

The Laundry Association ran advertisements urging women to send their laundry out. By doing so, they could save fifty-two laundry days. This time, the Association proclaimed, could be better invested "in the important business of keeping radiantly young and a real partner in your husband's happiness. For keeping young is a *Duty* in this youthful era."[103] Arch Preserver shoes adopted a similar advertising strategy. Their advertisement pictured a man and a woman playing golf above a bold-print caption which read "Again I am his Pal of Courtship Days." The testimonial which followed explained that the woman's husband wanted to golf and dance but she could not because she tired too quickly. She feared her husband would lose interest in her but fortunately her problem was solved by wearing Arch-Preserver shoes.[104]

Many advertisers used such youth-oriented scare tactics urging women to look young and slim or risk losing their husbands to other rivals. Advertisements for Camay soap, for example, warned women that they could not escape "the beauty contest of life...the rivalry of woman against woman." In this contest, the advertisement noted, the only useful weapon was beauty: especially fresh, radiant skin. These advertisements generally depicted elegant golf or tennis settings, yet warned that not even wealth or social position could help. Whether a woman lived "grandly in a mansion or modestly in a cottage," she could not escape the beauty contests. Someone's eyes were always judging her beauty, charm, and skin."[105]

One of the most unusual advertising campaigns using the sporting image was undertaken to save a faltering product. As the 1920s opened, Fleischmann's yeast faced plummeting sales as a result of the decline of home bread baking. Prohibition also contributed to this drop in sales by further limiting the demand for yeast. In desperation, Fleischmann's turned to the J. Walter Thompson advertising agency which transformed the product from a mere baking additive into a health food eaten directly out of the package.[106]

Those advertisements pictured men and women performing strenuous sports activities. They used actual photographs instead of the more impersonal artist's illustrations and further augmented the personal approach by using first-hand testimonials to Fleischmann's miraculous restorative powers. In 1927, for example, Fleischmann's advertisements contained the testimonial of a woman shown competing in an equestrian event who previously had been forced to give up all her beloved sports, even dancing, because of nerves. But after only five months of treatment (eating a cake of Fleischmann's yeast daily), she was again fit for any strenuous sport.[107]

A 1928 advertisement told the story of another woman who had always considered herself too delicate for athletics, but after Fleischmann's treatment was now playing tennis with great enthusiasm.[108] Even more impressive was the advertisement which ran that same year showing a woman in full mountain climbing gear scaling a steep rock face. The photograph's caption announced, "I was too weak for sports like this a few years back." But after Fleischmann's treatment, she enjoyed testing her new-found strength, in this case by making an ascent of Nisqually Glacier in Ranier National Park.[109] During the 1920s, Fleischmann's spent heavily on these advertisements and by 1926 had one of the nation's ten largest magazine advertising budgets. The campaigns, moreover, yielded spectacular results. By the spring of 1926, sales of Fleischmann's yeast had skyrocketed 130 per cent from 1923 when the campaign began.[110]

Corset makers fearing declining sales in the 1920s also hoped that advertising would cure their woes. Some companies responded by introducing less restrictive undergarments such as Lawrence Underwear or the heavily advertised Lady Sealpax which promised women the same comfortable loose-fitting underwear that men enjoyed, made specifically for the modern athletic woman.[111] Similarly, Treo introduced an elastic girdle called the Sportelete which they proclaimed as ideal for sports.[112]

By far, the most common tactic was to demonstrate that the traditional corset could function well in any circumstance without modification. Consequently, Spencer corsets printed the testimonial of a woman who claimed that her Spencer corset had helped her golf game. She noted that properly supported by a Spencer, she could play thirty-six holes of golf without tiring.[113] Similarly, Warner's corsets ran advertisement depicting women engaged in such activities as golf and tennis. The company promised that whatever activity a woman performed, her corset would withstand "every bend, lurch, or twist."[114]

Some companies took the drastic step of trying to scare women into buying their corsets. One of the most blatant advertising campaigns of this type was launched by the makers of PN Practical Front corsets. The advertisement featured a dejected looking woman watching other people dance. The caption read, "After the First Dance Does Your Husband Forget You?" In smaller print the advertisement asked, "What are your thoughts as he dances by, his arm about a younger woman? Does he even know that you are sitting out alone? Eternal call of Youth! What man can resist it? Your husband is no exception..." The corset company promised that their product could make this woman look younger and slimmer like magic. Then, she could send her husband, "an ever-fresh challenge: interesting, alluring, irresistible, fearing no rival."[115]

In a 1928 advertisement, the makers of Spencer corsets warned women to beware of the growing prevalence of fatter figures. They stated that eighty percent of all women had shown an increase in hip size of two to six inches because of the wearing of improper, non-supportive garments or because of the even worse habit of going without corsets altogether.[116] The company also made repeated appeals to elegance and to the importance of a youthful appearance. One advertisement in 1928 noted that all women, even "the debutante, spending long hours dancing or playing golf should have a Spencer designed to meet her individual needs as a most necessary youth insurance."[117] Also, in 1930, Spencer attempted to sell its product by telling women that it would restore their figures to youthful slenderness without exercise.[118]

Food advertisers also relied heavily on the sportswoman's image hoping to impart the idea that consumption of a certain food would produce vigor, energy, and sleek elegance. Many products emphasized their nutritional superiority, but many claims were rather dubious. Both Wrigley's Gum and Diamond Walnuts, for example, promised to improve the muscle tone of the face, by preventing flab and molding the lips prettily. After all, what good would exercise be if after achieving a better figure, a woman "let her face and neck grow old and lined?"[119]

Some food products made claims of increased athletic performance which were somewhat questionable. Chase and Sanborn coffee, showing an illustration of a man and woman engaged in archery, proclaimed that coffee drinkers made better athletes and had greater strength and endurance.[120] Schrafft's candy advertisements showing men and women playing golf or tennis praised their product for giving athletes quick energy. "You healthy golfers," began one advertisement, "eat a bite or two or three of Schrafft's when your drives begin to fall short."[121]

R.J. Reynolds Tobacco Company promoted their product, Camel cigarettes, by combining the promise of enhanced athletic performance with snob appeal. In a 1935 advertisement they introduced Mrs. Chiswell Dabney Langhorne who rode to the hounds in Albemarle County, Virginia. She remarked that she was very fond of Camel cigarettes because although they were not too strong, smoking one always picked her up if she tired.[122] In a long-running advertisement series Camel also promised women that smoking their cigarettes would preserve their youthful appearances by preventing the formation of a double chin.[123]

Some advertisers praised the time saving and healthful virtues of their products. The advertisements for Sara'ka laxatives, for example, were among the most unusual. Depicting a sporting scene (usually women playing golf or tennis), Sara'ka promised that by strengthening lazy intestinal muscles, its laxative gave men and women who had little time for outdoor sports a chance to be as healthy as an athlete.[124]

Nurtured by changing beauty standards which emphasized a slim youthful appearance and further reinforced by an emerging consumer movement which capitalized on the elegant, refined, and youthful look she projected, the sportswoman became a dominant cultural symbol. Some observers have pointed to the sportswoman as symbolic of the liberated woman of the 1920s. A stronger argument could be made, however, for the opposite interpretation. Throughout this period, a powerful and decidedly anti-feminist theme permeated the rhetoric of beauty. Beauty was no longer just a measure of healthful living, but instead a way to make certain that with the onslaught of middle-age, women would not lose their husbands to younger rivals.[125] Advertisers, mostly men, realizing that women did an estimated eighty-five per cent of retail buying, preached this message incessantly.[126]

Such attitudes were far from liberating for women and offered no challenge to the male-dominated world. On the surface, the dropping of age barriers for women in the area of personal appearance was liberating but it also created new restrictions. As Lois Banner has written, the normal attributes of old-age such as wrinkles, white hair, or sagging muscles were not seen as beautiful. What had changed rather was simply that the cultural prohibitions against older women attempting to look youthful were dropped. Mature women were not only free to diet and exercise, but it would seem, were required to do so.[127] In the words of one *Ladies' Home Journal* contributor, "any woman forty or so who looks her age is either stupid, or lazy, or both."[128]

The transition from the voluptuous to the athletic look took place during the first decades of the twentieth century. The transition appeared decisive and complete, and the older standard disappeared quickly. Throughout the 1920s, the image of the sportswoman seemed unshakable and destined for a long life. Surprisingly, this was not to be the case. Social movements already underway combined with the economic realities of the 1930s to expose the inherent weakness of America's acceptance of the sportswoman.

Chapter Five Notes

1. John Habberton, "Open-Air Recreation for Women," *Outing* (November 1889), pp. 160-161.

2. Harvey Levenstein, *Revolution at the Table, the Transformation of the American Diet* (New York: Oxford University Press, 1988), pp. 12-13. Levenstein cites Thomas Duncan, *How to Be Plump* (Chicago: Duncan Brothers, 1878).

3. Barbara Sicherman, "The Uses of a Diagnosis: Doctors, Patients and Neurasthenia," in Judith Walzer Leavitt and Ronald L. Numbers, eds. *Sickness and Health in America* (Madison: University of Wisconsin Press, 1985), p. 30. Sicherman cites from Massachusetts General Hospital Records, 1880-1900. See also S. Weir Mitchell, *Fat and Blood. An Essay on the Treatment of Certain Forms of Neurasthenia and Hysteria* (Philadelphia: Lippincott, 1888), and Mitchell, "Rest in Nervous Disorders," in E.C. Seguin, ed., *A Series of American Clinical Lectures* (New York: G.P. Putnam's Sons, 1875).

4. Janet Oppenheim, *Shattered Nerves. Doctors, Patients, and Depression in Victorian England* (New York: Oxford University Press, 1991).

5. Lois Banner, *American Beauty* (New York: Knopf, 1983).

6. Richmond Barrett, *Good Old Summer Days. Newport, Narragansett Pier, Saratoga, Long Beach, Bar Harbor* (Boston: Houghton-Mifflin, 1952), p. 192.

7. Banner, *American Beauty*, p. 136. *New York World* article cited by Banner is dated 1902.

8. Levenstein, *Revolution at the Table*, p. 14.

9. Barrett, *Good Old Summer Days*, pp. 192-194. See also Levenstein, *Revolution at the Table*, p. 13.

10. Banner, *American Beauty*, pp. 137-138.

11. *Ibid.*, p. 139.

12. Elizabeth Bisland, "Famous Beauties," *Cosmopolitan* (December 1889), p. 310.

13. *Ibid.*, p. 313.

14. *Ibid.*, p. 309.

15. Thiebault Sisson, "The Beautiful Models of Paris," *Cosmopolitan* (March 1895), p. 532.

16. Eleanor Waddle, "Side Glances at American Beauty," *Cosmopolitan* (June 1890), pp. 195-200. See also Bisland, "Famous Beauties," *Cosmopolitan* (December 1889), p. 306.

17. Banner, *American Beauty*, p. 203.

18. Harry Thurston Peck, "The Woman of Fascination," *Cosmopolitan* (November 1898), p. 76.

19. Nathalie Dana, *Young in New York: A Memoir of a Victorian Girlhood* (Garden City, N.J.: Doubleday, 962), p. 52.

20. Mrs. Burton Harrison, "Henley Week," *Cosmopolitan* (July 1900), pp. 361-362.

21. Cleveland Moffett, "Luxurious Newport," *Cosmopolitan* (August 1907), pp. 350, 358.

22. Harrison, "Henley Week," *Cosmopolitan* (July 1900), pp. 361-362.

23. Barrett, *Good Old Summer Days*, p. 43.

24. United States Lawn Tennis Association, *Fifty Years of Lawn Tennis in the United States* (New York: USLTA, 1931), p. 21.

25. Barrett, *Good Old Summer Days*, pp. 43-46.

26. *Ibid.*, p. 108.

27. Banner, *American Beauty*, p. 141.

28. Barrett, *Good Old Summer Days*, p. 112.

29. USLTA, *Fifty Years of Lawn Tennis*, p. 249.

30. Banner, *American Beauty*, p. 142.

31. Elizabeth Cynthia Barney, "The American Sportswoman," *Fortnightly Review* (August 1, 1899), p. 264.

32. Barrett, *Good Old Summer Days*, p. 43.

33. Barney, "The American Sportswoman," *Fortnightly Review* (August 1, 1899), p. 266.

34. Margaret Sangster, "From a Woman's Viewpoint," *Collier's* (June 16, 1900), p. 16.

35. Paulina Marietta Lyon, "The Only Woman's Athletic Club," *Collier's* (July 27, 1901), p. 23.

36. Barney, "The American Sportswoman," *Fortnightly Review* (August 1, 1899), p. 268.

37. Anna Wentworth Sears, "The Modern Woman Out-of-Doors," *Cosmopolitan* (September 1896), p. 630.

38. Sidney Cummings, "Lawn Tennis as a Health Builder," in William F. Fleming, ed., *Physical Culture Classics,* vol. 4 (New York: E.B. Dumont, 1909), p. 172.

39. Sears, "The Modern Woman Out-of-Doors," *Cosmopolitan* (September 1896), p. 638.

40. Barney, "The American Sportswoman," *Fortnightly Review* (August 1, 1899), p. 276.

41. Margaret Sangster, "From a Woman's Viewpoint," *Collier's* (April 13, 1901), p. 16; Sangster, "From a Woman's Viewpoint," *Collier's* (April 27, 1901), p. 18.

42. Bernarr Macfadden, "Building Vitality," in Fleming ed., *Physical Culture Classics,* vol. 2 (New York: E.B. Dumont, 1909), pp. 10, 20, 46.

43. Albert Treloar, *Treloars' Science of Muscular Development: A Textbook of Physical Training* (New York: Physical Culture Publishing Co., 1904), p. 10. See also Macfadden, *Muscular Power and Beauty* (New York: Physical Culture Publishing Co., 1906), pp. 20-21.

44. Macfadden, "Health Made and Preserved by Daily Exercise," *Cosmopolitan* (April 1903), p. 705.

45. Treloar, *Treloar's Science of Muscular Development*, p. 28.

46. Macfadden, "Health Made and Preserved," *Cosmopolitan* (April 1903), pp. 708, 712.

47. Macfadden, "The Development of Grace, Suppleness, and Symmetry," in Fleming ed., *Physical Culture Classics*, vol 4, p. 109.

48. James C. Whorton, "Patient Heal Thyself: Popular Health Reform as Unorthodox Medicine," in Norman Gevitz, ed., *Other Healers. Unorthodox Medicine in America* (Baltimore: Johns-Hopkins University Press, 1982), p. 78. The photographs Whorton mentions are found in Macfadden, *Womanhood and Marriage* (New York: Physical Culture Press, 1918), p. 12; and *The Power of Superb Womanhood* (New York: Physical Culture Press, 1901), p. 150.

49. Maude O'Dell, "Building a Physical Culture Girl," in Fleming, ed., *Physical Culture Classics*, vol. 4, pp. 106-107.

50. Whorton, "Patient Heal Thyself," p. 79.

51. *Ibid.*, p. 78.

52. Lapthorn Smith, M.D., "Higher Education of Women and Race Suicide," *Popular Science* (March 1905), p. 467.

53. Banner, *American Beauty*, p. 151.

54. Annette Kellerman, *Physical Beauty. How to Keep Fit* (New York: Geo. H. Doran, 1918), quote is from caption of photograph on frontispiece.

55. *Ibid.*, pp. 11-12.

56. *Ibid.*, pp. 13, 28.

57. *Ibid.*, p. 13.

58. *Ibid.*, pp. 15-16.

59. Banner, *American Beauty*, p. 146.

60. Grace Peckham Murray, M.D., "The Perils of Obesity," *Collier's* (June 29, 1901) p. 17.

61. Upton Sinclair,, "Starving for Health's Sake" *Cosmopolitan* (May 1910), p. 17.

62. Mrs. Woodrow Wilson, "The Woman of Fifty," *Cosmopolitan* (March 1903), pp. 503, 507.

63. H.M., "Growing Young Again," *Good Housekeeping* (February 1906), p. 231.

64. "Housework as an Aid to Health Culture," *Good Housekeeping* (December 1901), p. 509.

65. E. B. S., Kitchen Gymnastics," *Good Housekeeping* (January 1907), p. 118.

66. *Ibid.*, p. 119.

67. "Editorial," *Ladies' Home Journal* (November 1909), p. 6.

68. Dr. Lillian Bentley, "Dr. Bentley's Physical Culture for Girls," *Ladies' Home Journal* (November 1909), p. 27.

69. Dudley Sargent, "How Can I Have a Graceful Figure,? *Ladies' Home Journal* (February 1912), p. 15.

70. *Ibid.*

71. *Ibid.*

72. Dudley Sargent, "Are Athletics Making Women Masculine?" *Ladies' Home Journal* (March 1912), p. 72.

73. *Ibid.*, pp. 71-72.

74. *Ibid.*, p, 73.

75. Dudley Sargent, "After a Woman is Forty," *Ladies' Home Journal* (April 1912), p. 13.

76. *Ibid.*

77. Anna de Koven, "The Athletic Woman," *Good Housekeeping* (August 1912), pp. 148-149.

78. Levenstein, *Revolution at the Table* , p. 164. See also Banner, American Beauty, p. 165.

79. Advertisement for Grecian System of Physical Culture, *Ladies' Home Journal* (February 1903), p. 39. Unless otherwise noted, all advertisements below are from *Ladies' Home Journal*.

80. Advertisement for Grecian System of Physical Culture, (February 1904), p. 49.

81. Advertisement for Grecian System of Physical Culture, (February 1903), p. 39; (December 1902), p. 33.

82. Advertisement for "The Body Beautiful" booklet by Annette Kellerman, (May 1916), p. 95.

83. Advertisements for Susanna Cocroft, (June 1916), p. 70; (March 1920), p. 140.

84. Dana, *Young in New York*, p. 118.

85. Woods Hutchinson, M.D. "The Secret of Beauty," *Good Housekeeping* (March 1916), p. 329.

86. Dorothy Cooks, "Take Your Beauty Outdoors," *Ladies' Home Journal* (July 1934), p. 41.

87. Louise Paine Benjamin, "Sing or Swim," *Ladies' Home Journal* (July 1936), pp. 24-25.

88. Roland Marchand, *Advertising the American Dream. Making Way for Modernity, 1920-1940* (Berkeley: University of California Press, 1985), p. 6.

89. *Ibid.*

90. *Ibid.*

91. *Ibid.*, p. xxi.

92. Advertisement for Elgin Watches, (June 1925), p. 159.

93. Advertisement for Kotex Sanitary Napkins, (May 1929), p. 57.

94. Advertisements for Modess Sanitary Napkins, (March 1929), p. 77; (July 1929), p. 91; (April 1929), p. 105.

95. Marchand, *Advertising the American Dream*, p. xvii.

96. Advertisement for Vaseline Petroleum Jelly, (July 1929), p. 109.

97. Advertisement for Ford Automobiles, (April 1930), p. 91.

98. Advertisements for Cadillac Automobiles, (June 1928), p. 95; Buick, (July 1926), p. 91; Chrysler, (July 1928), p. 43; Dodge, (February 1927), p. 55; Overland, (December 1926), p. 55; Oldsmobile, (February 1927), p. 55.

99. Advertisement for Woodbury Soap, (July 1927), p. 31.

100. Advertisements for Woodbury Soap, (January 1927), p. 31; (May 1927), p. 43; (January 1926), p. 29.

101. Advertisement for *Ladies' Home Journal* (August 1928), pp. 76-77.

102. Advertisement for Palmolive Soap, (June 1927), p. 50.

103. Advertisement for Laundry Association, (October 1929), p. 123.

104. Advertisement for Arch-Preserver Shoes, (April 1927), p. 184.

105. Advertisements for Camay Soap, (June 1932), p. 2; (May 1933), p. 4.

106. Marchand, *Advertising the American Dream*, p. 16.

107. Advertisement for Fleishmann's Yeast, (October 1927), p. 65.

108. Advertisement for Fleischmann's Yeast, (June 1928), p. 43.

109. Advertisement for Fleischmann's Yeast (January 1928), p. 43.

110. Marchand, *Advertising the American Dream*, p. 16.

111. Advertisements for Lawrence Underwear, (March 1924), p. 205; Lady Sealpax Underwear, (November 1918), p. 55.

112. Advertisement for Treo Elastic Girdles, (April 1926), p. 100.

113. Advertisement for Spencer's Corsets, (March 1926), p. 172.

114. Advertisement for Warner's Corsets, (April 1920), p. 214.

115. Advertisement for PN Practical Front Corsets, (May 1927), p. 123.

116. Advertisement for Spencer's Corsets, (July 1928), p. 142.

117. Advertisement for Spencer's Corsets, (July 1928), p. 157.

118. Advertisement for Spencer's Corsets, (October 1930), p. 94.

119. Advertisement for Wrigley's Gum, (September 1930), p. 187. See also advertisement for Diamond Walnuts, (December 1933), p. 107.

120. Advertisement for Chase and Sanborn Coffee, (June 1933), p. 37.

121. Advertisement for Schrafft's Candy, (July 1931), p. 123.

122. Advertisement for Camel Cigarettes, (November 1935), p. 46.

123. Advertisement for Camel Cigarettes, *New York Times* (August 7, 1932), p. 23.

124. Advertisements for Sara'ka Laxative, (November 935), p. 46; (October 1935), p. 123; (December 1935), p. 83.

125. Banner, *American Beauty*, p. 207.

126. Marchand, *Advertising the American Dream*, p. 66.

127. Banner, *American Beauty*, pp. 224-225.

128. Ethel Lloyd Patterson, "Why Grow Old?" *Ladies' Home Journal* (July 1922), p. 7.

CHAPTER SIX

A Pendulum Swung Too Far? The Demise of the Sportswoman

"It is just now a nice question...whether the pendulum has not swung too far in the craze for unnatural physical exertion."[1]

Sportswriters have labelled the 1920s the golden age of American sports. It was the time of unprecedented popularity for professional baseball, golf, tennis, and football as many of the greatest athletes of all time captured the attention of the media and the public. Although the ideal of the sportswoman had assumed great prominence, any golden age for American women athletes was extremely short. While men's athletics produced such larger than life figures as Babe Ruth, Jim Thorpe, or Jack Dempsey, the sportswoman largely remained a symbol, an image depicting youth, glamour, and beauty. Aside from tennis champion Helen Wills Moody, and swimmer Gertrude Ederle, the sportswoman was, during the 1920s, more often a creation of advertising agencies than a real flesh and blood presence. As such, the sportswoman did not have a strong foundation of support and would not withstand the pressures brought by changing times and sentiments.

By far, the late 1920s and especially the Depression years of the 1930s proved to be the most critical in the downfall of the sportswoman. But opposition to many sports, especially those for women, actually pre-dated this time frame. A body of opinion dating back into the nineteenth century had long held that strenuous exercise was of dubious value. For example, education writer Kate Holladay Claghorn noted in 1897 that too many people endured gymnasium work because of the erroneous notion that muscular development was in itself a good thing. In keeping with the argument of a fixed amount of vital force, she warned that muscles were greedy. They would absorb for their own development all the nourishment afforded by the body. As a result, the exercising individual was left with a fatigued mind instead of the renewed strength and power expected.[2]

Writing for *Living Age* in 1899, Dr. Arabella Kenealy stated that she could not entertain the belief common to the uninformed laity that strenuous exercise promoted health. The public, she continued, operated on the mistaken belief that exercise resulted in a "material increase of force production." For Kenealy this was simply not the case. The human body, she explained, was like a machine with a fixed amount of operating force. The idea, therefore, that additional force could be created through exercise was a fallacy.[3]

Muscular development symbolized for some observers an imbalance. Unlike Macfadden or Kellerman, writers such as Kenealy and Claghorn did not make the connection between muscular development and health. According to Kenealy, muscular vigor was no test of health, either for men or women. She stated that it was common knowledge that athletes were the worst of all subjects for illness because the amount of energy needed to develop their physiques left them with little or no resistance to disease. Consequently, she claimed, athletes died proverbially young. She concluded that for women especially, any extreme muscle power was a clear sign of disease.[4] Writing for *Good Houskeeping*, Dr. Woods Hutchinson, a supporter of moderate exercise, lent his support to this line of thought declaring that too much exercise shortened life.[5]

A striking ambivalence surrounded the issue of exercise for women. For decades writers had extolled its virtues but many of them also issued warnings against excessive exertion. For example, Dr. J.M. Groedel wrote for *Good Housekeeping* that a certain amount of exercise served as an excellent preventative against heart ailments. Yet, he warned that over-exertion (especially sports) caused serious cardiac troubles.[6] A 1906 *Ladies' Home Journal* editorial concurred with this diagnosis, claiming that "the very best of our medical men are beginning seriously to think that young women are overdoing their athletics." The editorial noted that whereas exercise in general benefitted young women, "misdirected physical exercises" were injurious and "made for future invalidism." The author believed that serious trouble lay ahead for thousands of women if parents did not soon realize "what is going on and take the question of the exercise of their daughters firmly in hand."[7]

The critical point at the center of the debate was the question of limits. How much exercise was healthful and how much was too much? Most writers drew a strikingly fine line between healthful exercise and excessive training. Dr. Kenealy for example, was quite harsh in her assessment of most forms of exercise. While writing that within limits the heart could be "healthily stimulated and strengthened by exertion," she quickly qualified herself. She noted that physical activity increased the number of heart beats thereby reducing the rest that the heart enjoyed between beats. It was during these rests that the heart refreshed itself. With that in mind, she could not understand how any exercise more strenuous than walking could build vitality. She singled out cycling for special condemnation, proclaiming that the wheel would carry its master and especially its mistress to destruction. Cycling was a clear instance of over-exercise and had already led to an increase in gout among women and girls. Kenealy labelled nearly all forms of exercise as excessive believing instead that a day's rest would do more to restore and invigorate a person than any amount of athletics.[8]

Ladies' Home Journal also adopted the reasoning that if one had to breathe faster, the heart must also increase its beat. It proposed a simple method of recognizing the symptoms of diminishing returns. In a 1908 column, staff writer Emma Walker observed that if "during your exertion you are obliged to breathe through your mouth, you may be sure that your exercise is too strenuous."[9]

Physical culture promoter and writer Daniel Dowd, although far more enthusiastic on the subject of "athletic sports" than Kenealy, also stressed the importance of limits. He recommended that his readers should exercise only until they became "fairly tired." Thereafter, they should be careful to rest completely in order to recover strength. Any form of athletics which either pushed a person beyond the point of being fairly tired, or did not provide adequate rest periods was to be universally condemned.[10]

Still, the question remained, how much exercise was too much? At what point did one go beyond being just "fairly tired?" Because quantitative studies in the physiology of fatigue and stress lay years in the future, contemporary writers often expressed their varied objections to (and defenses of) exercise in largely qualitative terms. The American Medical Association, for example, endorsed the claim that strenuous exercise led to "heart strains that could last for days, or in extreme cases, for weeks."[11] In focusing on the effects of athletics on women's health, many writers continued to express the traditional and inordinate concern for women's child-bearing function. Because of widely-held beliefs that women were more prone to injury by over-exercising these rhetorical attacks on strenuous exercise were often directed against the alleged ill effects on women's reproductive systems, especially the uterus. In 1925, the *Journal of the American Medical Association* complained that in the "age of feminine freedom," common sense had become a lost commodity. Although not believing that menstruating girls should be coddled, the *Journal* did believe that athletics at such a time were a dangerous excess. There was no way of knowing, the author stated, how many girls on a basketball team scheduled to compete with another team on a given day were in the "midst of this feminine function in which the uterus was physiologically congested and temporarily abnormally heavy." In this condition the uterus was "liable to displacement by the inexcusable strenuosity and roughness of this particular game." The American Medical Association saw no need to place girls in such jeopardy because no prowess developed on the court could possibly be worth the risk.[12]

Alice Frymir, director of women's physical education at the University of Southern California, also concurred. In a training manual for physical education instructors published in 1930, Frymir continued to warn of the dangers of track and field. She argued strongly against any competition for women students during the menstrual cycle. By explanation, she noted that at this time the uterus was heavier than usual and "any jar may cause too great a pull on the ligaments sustaining this organ."[13] Similarly, *American Physical Education Review* author, E.H. Arnold, described track as a dangerous and unnatural activity that women would not attempt on their own unless they were pushed by an unwise coach.

He claimed that the rise of women's sport had caused abnormalities in the number, extent, and flow of the menses. Track and field had proven to be exceptionally hazardous, making the complete cessation of the menses a frequent and extensive occurrence. [14]

Athletic-induced amenorrhea loomed ominous for several reasons. Arnold believed it would lead to a sharp decline in fertility among American women. Furthermore, he stated that athletics would complicate childbirth. Proclaiming that "function makes the organ," he argued that athletics compressed the pelvis and diminished the size of the uterus. As a result, there would be an increase in the number of still-births and especially Caesarean section deliveries. He was horrified by what he saw as the exploitation of oncoming motherhood by athletics, branding competition as a menace to womanhood "the magnitude of which one can only contemplate with a shudder."[15]

Another great concern centered on the perceived emotional hazards of athletic competition. Many experts doubted that women possessed the emotional stamina to compete. On the issue of competitive sports, ambivalence gave way to more vocal opposition. Harriet Ballintine, for example, believed that her students needed a certain amount of excitement and an outlet for their exuberance. Yet while she advocated an hour or two of daily exercise, she roundly denounced all forms of competitive athletics, stating that "in the training of women, it is not physical overwork that is to be guarded against so much as nervous exhaustion."[16] The question of which activities were too strenuous was now clear. Exercise was fine; competition was a step too far.

Baron Pierre de Coubertin, the founder of the modern Olympic movement had long opposed any Olympic sports for women. He wrote that "no matter how toughened a sportswoman may be, her organism is not cut out to sustain certain shocks. Her nerves rule her muscles, nature wanted it that way." He did not believe that women's sports would be "an edifying sight" before the crowds assembled for an Olympiad. The only role women should play in the Olympics, he stated adamantly, would be to reward male athleticism with applause.[17] Interestingly, at the time which de Coubertin make these sharp comments, women only participated in golf, archery, tennis, and swimming in the summer

Olympics.[18] When women's track and field became an Olympic sport in 1928, the furor over women's participation would reach a crescendo.

Another major objection to sports for women centered on the effects of competition on feminine character. Many writers believed that competitive athletics had destroyed the finer womanly traits. Kenealy argued that "the power of a healthy adult can be increased only at the expense of some other power." In this case, the modern woman had inordinately added to her muscle-power, but only at the expense of higher, more valuable factors. Just as the Biblical figure of Esau had bartered way his birth-right, women had bartered away all their fine qualities for muscles. In her opinion, the lean and muscular female body, far from being beautiful, was an insult to nature. She believed that the most beautiful women were to be found among the women of the South who did not exercise, scarcely walked, and yet displayed "the most beautiful rounding of form." The modern woman, she lamented, was not only muscular, but also loud, assertive, selfish, callous, and immodest.[19]

This lack of modesty was a recurring charge levelled against the sportswoman. Earlier, for example, *Good Housekeeping* had printed an editorial denouncing what it called "*the spirit of unwise freedom at sports*," which was "asserting itself strongly in the matter of dress which women don at their athletics." The editorial stated that no one would for a moment criticize a woman for wearing a dress which would give her more freedom of movement. But it quickly condemned garments "so scant as to leave the limbs exposed." There was no possible excuse for a grown woman to forget herself, her years, and her sex and to parade in short skirts. The editorial defined short as being eight inches above the sweep line.[20] This criticism of the sportswomen would only escalate as the years passed and athletic attire became steadily shorter.

Similarly, many physical educators assessing the development of women's sports were not pleased at what they saw. Writing in 1906 for the *American Physical Education Review*, Frances Kellor wrote that she had always believed that athletic sports for women should stress the aesthetic values such as beauty, grace, carriage, and a neat, attractive appearance. But looking out upon a playing field or court it was clear that these values were not on display. Instead, the saddened observer would see only "disagreeable expressions, uncouth language, squealing, yelling, lying about the floor, masculinity, and boisterousness." The fighting characteristics of competition had, it seemed, led to the development of aggressive characteristics which were not in harmony with the "best traditions of the sex."[21]

Some writers at the turn of the century tried to comfort their readers with the hope that the sportswoman would soon go out of style. As *Cosmopolitan* stated, many people complained about the cycling and golfing girl who, "eats like a coal heaver, drinks highballs, and carries a cigarette case in the pocket of her Norfolk jacket." Nevertheless, the author predicted, "this type will pass when the fashion changes." Already, there were signs that a strong reaction had set in against what the author labelled "unnecessary and odious mannishness."[22]

Likewise, *Good Housekeeping* also believed that the sportswoman would eventually lose her appeal. The magazine noted in 1910 that a young man's fancy turned currently only to the girl who is a "good pal, who has made the college basket-ball team, and who puts up a stiff game of tennis." His fancy would, however, change and after his infatuation with the athlete he would naturally seek the opposite type of woman and find her "all fluffy frills and feminine charms."[23]

To many observers, competitive sports for women were not only damaging to health and femininity, but simply unnecessary or insignificant. Dr. Luther Gulick, writing for the *American Physical Education Review* in 1906, stated that athletics had no relationship whatsoever to womanhood. Prehistoric men may have survived based on their ability to run and throw, but not women. Athletic feats provided no measure of womanhood.[24] Even Dudley Sargent, a strong advocate of some forms of exercise for women, denounced competitive athletics, believing that an outstanding woman athlete was a contradiction in terms. He noted that women were handicapped by nature for effective sports competition. Any woman who did in fact excel in sports must possess certain inherited masculine traits such as broad shoulders or narrow hips. For Sargent, a woman could be athletic or feminine, but not both.[25]

Many writers expressed the belief that women could never become truly great athletes. Edith Rickert, writing for *Ladies' Home Journal*, announced that any woman "lost in the keenness of competition" was wasting her time in a futile attempt to imitate men. At best, all she could hope for was to become a second-rate athlete. College women especially should learn their physical limitations and be content with physical education which would make them strong and able to bear the strains of life after college.[26]

By far, the most vocal champion of this argument was noted sportswriter and novelist Paul Gallico. He stated that women simply could not be taken seriously at their games because they were at best second-rate imitations of men and could never be good enough to matter. Whatever public appeal women athletes possessed must be attributed to sex appeal. He noted bluntly that the female form in any manner of undress sold newspapers. The more revealing the outfit, the more popular the sport. He believed that the sport of swimming proved his point. According to Gallico, male swimmers were faster and better, but no one bothered to go and see them compete or print their pictures in the paper.[27]

Gallico also believed, as did Sargent, that the best women athletes possessed masculine traits. He described the most successful woman athlete of his day, Mildred "Babe" Didrickson, as a "muscle-moll." She was "hard-bitten, hawk-nosed, and thin-mouthed with essentially a boy's body." She was driven, Gallico claimed, by a strong dislike and contempt for all things feminine. As he described, women such as Didrickson, flat-chested, with hard and knotty muscles, took to sport readily to escape and to compensate for whatever it was they lacked in sex appeal. According to Gallico, when Didrickson gave up track and field and took up the more sedate game of golf, her demeanor changed. As she began to attract men, she let her hair grow and began wearing make-up. The last time he had seen her, she sported a "stylish hair wave and an attractive sports ensemble complete with matching purse."[28]

As many observers debated the proper amount of exercise or the suitability of competition for women, another important development in the demise of the sportswoman occurred within the ranks of academic physical education. The profession had long debated how much exercise was enough and which sports were appropriate for their women students. Disagreements were not uncommon, but by the 1920s, physical educators had begun to solidify their position, supporting athletics as a source of exercise and fun, but frowning upon organized games and especially competitive events.

Many instructors believed that competitive sports had perverted the true course of physical education. Physical education, they argued, should be available to everyone. As the oft-repeated phrase stated, it should provide "the greatest good for the greatest number." Varsity sports, however, were blatantly undemocratic. Under the varsity system, coaches chose a small group of girls representing a minuscule percentage of the student body to compete and then gave them their undivided attention. The great irony was that these select few did not need the extra training to achieve the desired level of fitness. The attention of physical educators would be better spent promoting activities for all students rather than for a limited number chosen for their physical prowess.[29]

If action were not taken immediately, the professionals claimed, dire consequences would follow. Athletics would otherwise lose much of its value. Helen Coops, head of the Physical Education Department at the University of Cincinnati, warned in 1926 of this dangerous trend. She believed that if the overdevelopment of a small group and the "absolute neglect of the greater majority of girls" continued, then the play spirit would be lost and with it, "all character training and general development." The sad result would be do-or-die competition in which students would be "proud and happy to break a blood vessel if they could break a record along with it."[30]

Something must be done to ensure that the spirit of wholesome play for all girls would not be sacrificed. Sports had to be conducted for the good of all and not simply for the purpose of building championship teams.[31] The solution, as described by Dorothy Ainsworth in her 1930 history of women's physical education, came in the form of "play days." Common by the late 1920s, play days were an extension of intramural sports in which women from several colleges, schools, or classes were mixed together to play a variety of sports.[32] Experts throughout the profession praised the new sports format. Writing for the

Carnegie Foundation for the Advancement of Teaching, Howard Savage lauded the concept. In his opinion, play days removed the undesirable aspects of acute competition and fostered friendship.[33]

Similarly, Agnes Wayman of Barnard College was gladdened by the sight of the new play days. She had long believed that victories in competitive sports contests meant very little, either from a sport or a health viewpoint. As she explained, having a girls' basketball team from New York beat a team from Chicago was basically meaningless. Far more significant would be to have a larger percentage of girls participating in properly supervised fitness activities in New York than in Chicago. That was the idea that must be sold to the public. Wayman stated that the most spectacular thing she could think of would be for some public-spirited person to donate one million dollars and then to stipulate that the sum was not for a huge stadium where seventy-five thousand people would watch twenty-two men playing football. Instead, the money would go to build athletic fields and gymnasiums where a few would superintend the playing of thousands.[34]

As the play day format became accepted by most women's physical education instructors, almost all forms of inter-collegiate competition ceased. This level of unanimity can be attributed to the organizational structure of women's colleges. Unlike the situation at men's colleges, few departments of physical education for women separated the three functions of teacher preparation, general physical education, and extra-curricular recreation and sport into different staff responsibilities. The same people who ran the sports programs also conducted the teacher education programs and thus were able to indoctrinate the teachers-to-be in this national philosophy.[35]

Professional physical educators, therefore, exercised great hegemony over their collegiate programs. Yet, much of the growth in women's sports at this time took place outside the academic realm and consequently free from their control. Throughout the 1920s, sporting activities for women mushroomed as large industrial concerns, banks, chambers of commerce, and non-collegiate athletic clubs sponsored leagues and events. The physical education profession saw this development as the epitome of evil and roundly denounced it. Physical educators condemned all such contests for exploiting women in return for publicity or money. They claimed that women athletes were being pushed beyond themselves physically and emotionally to satisfy sponsors and crowds.[36] In a letter to her counterpart at the University of Kentucky, Anna Norris, head of women's physical education at the University of Minnesota, wrote that if such exploitive events continued, women athletes would be "butchered to make a Roman holiday" in the tradition of the ancient gladiators.[37]

Exaggerated accounts of the horrors of unscientific and unsanctioned competitions filled the pages of many physical education journals. Helen Coops, for example, told of a ghastly women's basketball tournament where men jeered at the women players who were attired in "abbreviated costumes." The pace of the game was so great that several women had to be removed from the floor in fainted or hysterical conditions. The crowd urged the remaining competitors on with shouts of "Fight! Fight!"[38]

Noted sports writer John Tunis recalled a similar tale in 1929 for his *Harper's Monthly* readers. His description of a woman's industrial league basketball tournament sounded like a passage from Dante. The contest took place in a dark gymnasium made even darker by the thick cigarette smoke which defeated the windows' attempts to admit light. To make matters worse, the windows were closed in clear violation of the sacred principle of proper ventilation. In this foul and suffocating arena, women played in a "brittle state of taut excitement." Before long, one of the players, apparently weaker than the others, collapsed completely. After being carried into the dressing room she became "racked by hysteria, her body tightly drawn into a knot." She was a nervous invalid, Tunis diagnosed. She would recover physically, but her nervous suffering was so acute that many weeks would pass before she regained her complete health.[39]

Physical educators urged that for the safety of women the management of women's sports must be left to them. They had great reservations about competition, even when conducted "under ideal health supervision." But now the situation was intolerable. Untrained men (in the form of coaches) were responsible for the health of the American girl. They were not, the professionals argued, properly trained for the task. They had not received the necessary training in college and as a result did not teach physical training so much as physical straining.[40] A favorite tactic used by many physical education writers involved horrific stories of the barbaric training programs imposed upon male athletes by untrained and unscientific coaches. Tales abounded of "long and killing runs before breakfast," diets limited to oatmeal and raw meat, and athletes deprived of water during training to harden them for competition.[41] The only proper solution was to place the whole matter of women's athletics in the hands of trained professionals who understood the needs and limits of women's physiology.[42]

Developments in men's collegiate sports further alarmed those women's physical education instructors who were already fearful of losing control of their discipline to outside forces. The rise of men's intercollegiate athletics had brought with it independent athletic departments governed by coaches and athletic directors. Furthermore, athletic contests moved out of the gymnasiums and into public arenas beyond the control of physical education departments. As those events, especially collegiate football, became popular, drawing huge paying crowds, the balance of power shifted. Such a situation in women's sports was to be avoided at all costs and, it could be argued, this motivation fueled many of the attacks against competitive sports for women.

Defenders of women's physical education drew considerable support from a general anti-sports movement which had been gaining momentum since the 1880s. At the heart of this movement were sharp attacks on men's amateur sports, especially in colleges. Many writers believed that men's collegiate sports should be abolished because of rampant professionalism and corruption and in the case of football, brutality.[43]

By the time the 1920s arrived, men's collegiate programs had received so much negative publicity that the prestigious Carnegie Foundation for the Advancement of Teaching commissioned studies. The reports condemned men's collegiate sports noting that too many outside influences and too much outside money had corrupted college athletics. Colleges were urged to take control of their programs and return sport to non-competitive and less exclusive amateur ideals. To do so, athletic directors, coaches, scholarships, training tables, as well as surreptitious loans, gifts, and jobs granted to athletes must be abolished. The well-being of the colleges, the student body, and sport in general demanded that these corrupting outside influences be eliminated.[44]

With men's collegiate athletics in disrepute, it was easier for women's physical educators to denounce competitive sports. While some experts reasoned that women must be safeguarded against the corruption of men's programs, others, in a variation of the nineteenth century argument about women's moral superiority, contended that women should withdraw from sports in order to persuade men to do so.[45] Mabel Lee, president of the American Physical Education Association, urged her colleagues to maintain the integrity of their programs. "May the time never come," she implored, "when the ideals of athletics for women are thrown to the winds as ideas have been in men's athletics."[46]

In this unpromising environment, the 1928 Olympic games took place giving critics of women's sports powerful ammunition to use in their campaigns against competitive sports. In that year, women's track and field made its debut as an Olympic event. Over two hundred and fifty women competed in the Olympic trials held in New York in July. Nineteen were selected for the team. Of that number, eighteen received sponsorship from non-collegiate athletic clubs, including four from the renowned Milrose Athletic Association of New York.[47]

Reports which filtered back from the Olympic games at Amsterdam reveal a striking level of antagonism on the part of the sportswriters. The women's one hundred meter dash, for example, was described as "the most interesting event on the program inasmuch as it provided, aside from the race itself, other scenes entirely feminine and never before witnessed in an Olympic stadium."[48]

As the runners took their marks, the reporter noted, they all appeared extremely nervous and jumpy. Two competitors were in fact disqualified for false-starts. One of the two women responded by shouting and shaking her fist at the official starter. According to the New York Times, it seemed for a moment that she might confront the starter and "stage a face-scratching and hair-pulling act." While this protest continued, the other disqualified runner, described as "a slight, attractive lass wearing red shorts and a white silk blouse," sat down on the track and burst into tears. In doing so, she blocked the path of the other runners and had to be carried, still sobbing, into the infield "where she remained, her head buried in her arms and her body shaking with sobs for at least a half an hour."[49]

In that report, those writers who had opposed women's sports saw proof that women could not compete at high levels because of the undue stress it placed upon their nerves. The one hundred meter run was not, however, the most dramatic or controversial event of the Amsterdam Olympiad. That distinction went to the women's eight hundred meter race, a distance thought by many at that time to be a long distance event for women. Accounts of that race served as a ringing denouncement of women's athletics. The *New York Times* reported that even though German runner Lina Radke set a world's record, the race plainly demonstrated that the distance made, "too great a call on feminine strength." At the finish, the paper noted, six of nine runners were completely exhausted and "fell headlong on the ground." Several runners had to be carried off the track.[50]

John Tunis offered an even more exaggerated account of the race. Anyone, he wrote, who still believed that women could stand the strain of athletic competition should have stood beside him during the running of the women's eight hundred meter final. He noted that on the cinder track were "eleven wretched women, five of whom dropped out before the finish, while five collapsed after reaching the tape." He was informed later that the event's sole survivor fainted in the dressing room shortly after the race.[51] Tunis' story and especially his arithmetic were indeed suspect. According to official records, only nine women ran in the eight hundred meter final, not eleven. Additionally, only two runners, failed to finished the race, not five.[52]

Some reports suggested that such tales of carnage were unfounded and were probably written to tarnish the participation of women. There was, however, some disagreement. Mary Traynor Washburn, for example, gave a report far different from the *Times*. Washburn, a silver medalist on the United

States four hundred meter relay team and spectator at the eight hundred meter final, stated that no one collapsed. Furthermore, one official at the scene reported that three women collapsed. The public and journalists, he noted, believed them to be in a state of exhaustion. He was judging the event and claimed to the contrary that "there was nothing wrong with them, they burst into tears, thus betraying their disappointment at having lost the race."[53]

These accounts went unheeded amid the simmering disapproval of women's athletics. Physical educators used such exaggerated reports to strengthen their condemnation of women's sports programs. The National Amateur Athletic Federation of the United States also used the negative and distorted publicity of the eight hundred meter race as part of its rationale for lobbying against all Olympic events for women. The issue was hotly debated at the Congress of International Athletic Federation in August, 1928. Although some nations wanted to abolish all women's contests, the governing body decided to drop only the eight hundred meter race for women and retain the other events. In addition, a new event would be added to the next Olympiad: the women's eighty meter hurdles.[54]

Women athletes in previous Olympiads had not generated such hostilities. Two reasons can be given to explain why track and field attracted so much criticism. First, by attacking track and field, physical educators were also attacking the rival organization, the Amateur Athletic Union, which in 1922 had taken control of track further galvanizing the physical education community.[55] Second, unlike such competitors in sports such as golf, tennis, or crew, track and field athletes (especially women) were often sponsored by non-collegiate athletic clubs such as the Milrose Athletic Association funded by a New York department store, or the Employers Casualty Athletic Association of Dallas underwritten by a Texas insurance agency and made famous by it sponsorship of the 1932 Olympic star Mildred "Babe" Didrickson.[56]

Track and field lacked the aristocratic country club heritage of golf and tennis. Its participants generally did not adorn magazine covers or appear in product advertisements. Moreover, women's colleges did not train Olympic track stars, remaining firm in the belief that sports were a form of recreation for all. The women who would, therefore, provide the material for the Olympic teams every four years came from factories, offices, and shops.[57] Track and field's identification with the working class and lower class continued for decades, ensuring that its appeal would remain limited.

Professional physical education's withdrawal of support from competitive sports for women was of great importance, but it was hardly the only cause of the decline in the sportswoman's appeal. The image of the sportswoman had risen to great heights in the 1920s independent of (if not actually contrary to) professional physical education. It could, therefore, have continued without that support had other events not taken place as well. The sportswoman's great appeal had centered around her identification with leisure, consumerism, and refined living. The Great Depression would sweep these away.

A backlash against the activities of the 1920s was noticeable during the Depression. *Ladies' Home Journal* editorials bear this out. In a 1932 editorial, the magazine stated that it was glad the "jazz decade of the 1920s with its bad manners and indifferent morals" was quickly disappearing and a new saner and stronger America was arising. The editors also blasted another prominent trend of the 1920s which they labeled "the cult of the body." Under the guise of beauty, the editors complained, the practically unclothed woman had begun to creep into public print, stage, and pictures. Those irresponsible days were now gladly gone, and the youth who so alarmed the country ten years ago no longer caused anxiety.[58]

The sportswoman was closely linked with those irresponsible days. *Ladies' Home Journal* had already blasted the athletic woman as a major part of a frivolous age. She was a "powder-puff pet" who used birth control and preferred to lounge ingloriously at the country club, guzzle boot-leg cocktails, and talk everlastingly about sex and divorce. Barton S. Curie, author of this editorial, stated that real women were those who could point with pride to the size of their families and the efficiency of their homes.[59] The sportswoman's association with youth, sex appeal, and modernity, once so beneficial, had become a grave liability.

By far, the most damaging effect of the Depression upon the appeal of the sportswoman was economic. During these years, fewer women had the leisure time for sports, or the money to join country clubs or attend college. Deprived of sponsorship, many of the industrial leagues withered. The effects of the Depression were also acutely felt by the advertising industry. Those advertisers which during the 1920s had relied on the sportswoman's appeal to sell their products found their budgets slashed. With fewer clients, advertising agencies could not continue their campaigns, and the sheer volume of advertising in popular magazines plummeted. As a result, the sportswoman, once a prominent feature in advertising, lost considerable visibility. Magazines which relied on those advertising dollars either went out of business or published abbreviated issues. *Ladies' Home Journal* chose the latter option. Its issues of 1928 averaged 208 pages per monthly magazine. By 1933, the issues had shrunk to an average of 119 pages.

Additionally, many advertisers which had used the sportswoman in their 1920s campaigns changed strategies for the 1930s. In the following table, an analysis of advertisements from *Ladies' Home Journal* (a magazine with a reported circulation of over three million copies per month) points to the declining importance of the sportswoman in Depression-era advertising. Advertisements depicting women engaged in sports were a phenomenon of the 1920s. The period 1920-1925 saw more than a fifty-five percent increase over the previous five year period. The late twenties witnessed a similar increase. Thereafter, the number of such advertisements began to decline, falling sharply by the end of the 1930s (See Table 2).

Table 2.
Advertisements Depicting Women in Sports,
Ladies' Home Journal, 1901-1940

Year	Number of Advertisements
1901-1905	16
1906-1910	6
1911-1915	11
1916-1920	66
1921-1925	102
1926-1930	145
1931-1935	69
1936-1940	33

During the Depression, the sportswoman virtually disappeared from the advertisements of popular magazines. Hinds' lotion, for example, had advertised in the 1920s that its product soothed hands roughened by tennis. But in the 1930s, it soothed hands damaged by housework.[60] As advertised in the 1920s, Fleischmann's yeast miraculously gave invalids the strength to perform heroic athletic deeds. In the 1930s, it advertised that it helped thin children grow. Fleischmann's also paid twenty-five dollars for testimonials from adults over forty years of age, but no epic tales of athletic exploits ensued.[61] The makers of Woodbury's soap also abandoned their country club sports campaigns of the 1920s. After an unusual campaign featuring unclothed women, Woodbury's built its late 1930s campaign around socialites and debutantes who, after being freshened by their soap, went to parties, not to tennis courts or golf courses.[62]

For some companies, the emerging Hollywood film star replaced the sportswoman in 1930s advertising campaigns. Lux soap, for example, claimed that it was the choice of beautiful screen stars. Many famous stars did appear in Lux advertisements, including Bette Davis, Claudette Colbert, Dorothy Lamour, Carole Lombard, and Barbara Stanwyck.[63] Other companies followed the example of Lux. As a result, Joan Bennett endorsed Jergens lotion, while Ginger Rogers extolled the virtues of Double Mint chewing gum.[64]

Advertisers in the 1930s still warned women to beware of losing or not catching a man, but a change had taken place over a decade. Unlike the 1920s advertisements, there was no mention of the importance of sport for keeping a youthful appearance. In the 1920s, for example, Arch-Preserver Shoes noted in an advertisement that it could solve the problems of the woman who was so tired at the end of the day that she could not go golfing with her husband and as a result he was losing interest in her. A decade later, Arch-Preserver promised it could solve the similar difficulty of a woman so tired by day's end that she did not want to go to the movies with her husband.[65]

Advertisements for Franco-American spaghetti followed a similar line of reasoning. Franco-American claimed that its product could make housework easier so that after a day's work, wives would still have enough pep to go to the movies with their husbands.[66] Similarly, the makers of Coco-Malt beverage mix noted that men expected much more of a wife than formerly. It was not enough to keep a good house. She "must be wife, mother, sweetheart, and pal all rolled into one, ready to 'go places' at a moment's notice." Fortunately, Coco-Malt contained "one and three-quarters hours of energy in every glass" so even after hours of housecleaning she would be ready.[67]

Product advertisements in the 1930s were replete with sad tales of women who could not attract men. Unlike the advertisement of the 1920s, however, the 1930s message was, it seems, not to look athletic but rather to smell better. Mum deodorant preached the supreme importance of personal "daintiness." In bold print heading, one Mum advertisement that dramatized a social event proclaimed, "They crowded around for introduction, but they only danced one dance." The horrifying mistake of this would-be debutante at this dance was that although she "carefully bathed and dressed, she neglected one simple precaution and trusted her bath alone to keep her safe from underarm odor, Fatal error." A girl who wanted a second dance or date used Mum.[68]

Mum also warned married women of the importance of daintiness. It told several stories of husbands who had lost interest in their wives. Under the heading "How Many Kisses Does a Good Wife Miss?" a Mum deodorant advertisement explained that the wife was actually at fault for the husband's lack of interest. Although she might be shocked to know it, "any woman should realize it takes more than a bath to keep underarms fresh and sweet."[69]

Lux laundry soap employed a similar advertising campaign, noting that "charming wives *never* risk offending, especially with nighties that have perspiration odor."[70] In a 1938 advertisement, Lux told the sad story of a neglected wife. She complained that her husband had lost interest in her and kissed her in a bored manner "like a woodpecker tapping a tree." He also went to bed too early and was snoring even before she could get undressed. The husband explained to the *Ladies' Home Journal* readers that he still loved his wife but she was no longer dainty. Worst of all, she wore lingerie that did not "smell attractive."[71]

Some advertisers adopted entirely different tactics to deal with the realities of the Depression. Chase and Sanborn coffee, which in the 1920s advertised that it gave steady energy to athletes, now boasted in the 1930s that because it was sold in bags, it cost less than other brands sold in cans. The price difference prompted the woman in the advertisement to exclaim, "I'm proud of the savings I can show in my household accounts." [72] Similarly, Chrysler automobiles dropped its country club appeals and announced that it had invaded the low-priced field.[73]

The 1920s may well have been the golden age of sports, but the Great Depression brought an end to what some scholars have labelled "the first wave of athletic feminism."[74] There was less time for leisure, less money for clubs, and fewer opportunities for college. Sports and recreation programs for women were canceled, scaled down, or under-funded for a variety of ideological as well as economic reasons. Robbed of academic backing and advertising appeal, the sportswoman disappeared, lost in the feminine mystique of enforced motherhood and domesticity which so dominated the 1940s, 1950s, and 1960s.

Chapter Six Notes

1. Are Girls Overdoing Athletics?" *Ladies' Home Journal* (May 1906), p. 16.
2. Kate Holladay Claghorn, *College Training for Women* (New York: Thomas Crowell, 1897), p. 114.
3. Arabella Kenealy, "Woman As Athlete," *Living Age* (April 29, 1899), p. 363.
4. *Ibid.*, p. 365.
5. Woods Hutchinson, M.D., "The Bugbear of Exercise," *Good Housekeeping* (December 1913), p. 41.
6. Dr. J.M. Groedel, "How to Avoid Heart Troubles," *Good Housekeeping* (January 1901), p. 41.
7. "Are Girls Overdoing Athletics," *Ladies' Home Journal* (May 1906), p. 16. See also Edith Rickert, "Has the College Injured the Health of Girls?" *Ladies' Home Journal* (January 1912), p. 12.
8. Kenealy, "Woman as Athlete. A Rejoinder," *Living Age* (July 22, 1899), pp. 204, 209-210.
9. Emma Walker, "Pretty Girl Questions," *Ladies' Home Journal* (October 1908), p. 54.
10. Daniel Dowd, *Physical Culture for Home and School, Scientific and Practical* (New York: Fowler-Wells, 1888), p. 27.
11. "Athletic Strenuosity," *Journal of the American Medical Association* (July 1925), p. 270, reprinted in "Extracts, Abstracts, and Notice of Magazine Articles," *American Physical Education Review* (July 1925), p. 524.
12. *Ibid.*
13. Alice Frymir, *Track and Field for Women* (New York: Barnes, 1930), p. 22.
14. E.H. Arnold, "Athletics for Women," *American Physical Education Review* (October 1924), pp. 452-455.
15. *Ibid.*, pp. 454, 457.
16. Harriet Ballintine, "Out-of-Door Sports for College Women," *American Physical Education Review* (March 1898), p. 41.
17. Cited in Ellen Gerber, et. al., *The American Woman in Sport* (Reading, Mass.: Addison-Wesley, 1974), pp. 137-138. Passage cited is from two quotes dated 1910 and 1912 respectively.
18. *Ibid.*, p. 147.
19. Kenealy, "Woman as Athlete," *Living Age* (April 29, 1899), p. 363; Kenealy, Woman as Athlete. A Rejoinder," *Living Age* (July 22, 1899), p. 210.

20. "Editorial: The Side That's Close to the Sun," *Ladies' Home Journal* (May 1898), p. 3.

21. Frances Kellor. "Ethical Value of Sports for Women," *American Physical Education Review* (September 1906), p. 163. See also Mabel Lee, "A Consideration of the Fundamental Differences Between Boys and Girls as they Affect the Girls' Problems of Physical Education." *Education* (April 1933), p. 468.

22. Rafford Pyke, "Strength in Women's Features," *Cosmopolitan* (November 1904), p. 111. See also Henry T. Finck, "Are Womanly Women Doomed?" *Independent* (January 31, 1901), pp. 267-268.

23. "A Young Man's Fancy," *Good Housekeeping* (April 1910), p. 424.

24. Dr. Luther Halsey Gulick, "Athletics Do Not Test Womanliness," *American Physical Education Review* (September 1906, pp. 158-159.

25. Dudley Sargent, "What Athletic Games are Injurious to Women," *American Physical Education Review* (September 1906), pp. 176-177.

26. Edith Rickert, "Has College Injured the Health of Girls?" *Ladies' Home Journal* (January 1912), pp. 11-12.

27. Paul Gallico, *Farewell to Sports* (New York: Knopf, 1938), pp. 235, 239-242, 244, 250.

28. *Ibid.*, p. 240.

29. "Outstanding Problems of Girls' Athletics," *American Physical Education Review* (May 1926), p. 846.

30. Helen Coops, "Sports for Women," *American Physical Education Review* (November 1926), p. 1096. See also Woods Hutchinson, M.D., "The Bugbear of Exercise," *Good Housekeeping* (December 1913), p. 822.

31. Gerber, et. al., *The American Woman in Sport*, p. 147.

32. Dorothy Ainsworth, *The History of Physical Education in Colleges for Women* (New York: A.S. Barnes, 1930), p. 85.

33. Howard J. Savage, et. al., *Current Developments in American Sport* (New York: Carnegie Foundation for the Advancement of Teaching, Bulletin 26, 1931), p. 7.

34. Agnes Wayman, "Women's Athletics: All Uses, No Abuses," *American Physical Education Review* (November 1924), p. 518.

35. Gerber, et. al., *The American Woman in Sport*, pp. 63, 67. See also Gerber, "The Controlled Development of Collegiate Sport for Women," *Journal of Sport History* (Spring 1975), p. 9.

36. Stephanie L. Twin, ed., *Out of the Bleachers, Writings on Women and Sport* (Old Westbury, N.Y.: Feminist Press, 1979), p. xxx.

37. Anna Norris to Sarah Blanding, Undated Letter, Sarah Blanding Papers, Physical Education File, Special Collections, M.I. King Library North, University of Kentucky, Lexington, Kentucky.

38. Coops, "Sports for Women," *American Physical Education Review* (November 1926), p. 1088.

39. John Tunis, "Women and the Sport Business," *Harper's Monthly* (July 1929), p. 214.

40. Mabel Lee, "The Case For and Against Intercollegiate Athletics for Women and the Situation as it Stands To-day," *American Physical Education Review* (January 1924), p. 15.

41. Jay Nash, "Athletics for Girls, " *North American Review* (January 1928), p. 100. See also "Is Athletic Training Overdone?" *Illustrated Sporting News* (March 5, 1904), p. 1.

42. "Outstanding Problems of Girls' Athletics," American Physical Education Review (May 1926), p. 846.

43. C.A. Young, "College Athletic Sports, *Forum* (October 1886), pp. 146-147; "Editors' Study," *Forum* (November 1893), pp. 961-962; William DeWitt Hyde, "A Rational System of Physical Training," *Forum* (June 1891), p. 446; Arlo Bates, "The Negative Side of Modern Athletics," *Forum* (May 1901), p. 290, 297.

44. Savage, et. al., *Current Developments in American Sports*, pp. 34-36.

45. Lois Banner, *American Beauty* (New York: Knopf, 1983), p. 286.

46. Cited in Gerber, "The Controlled Development of Collegiate Sport for Women," *Journal of Sport History* (Spring 1975), p. 20. Quote is from *New York Times* (April 2, 1931), p. 32.

47. "Miss Cartwright Wins Three Titles," *New York Times* (July 5, 1928), p. 15.

48. "United States Captures Two Olympic Events," *New York Times* (August 1928), p. 1.

49. *Ibid.*, p. 16.

50. Wythe Williams, "Americans Beaten in Four Olympic Tests," *New York Times* (August 3, 1928), p. 3.

51. Tunis, "Women and the Sports Business," *Harper's Monthly* (July 1929), p. 213.

52. Barry Hugman, ed., *The Olympic Games. Complete Track and Field Results, 1896-1988* (New York: Facts on File, 1988), p. 104.

53. Judith Jenkins George, "Mary Washburn Conklin, Pioneer in Women's Olympic Track and Filed," *Journal of Physical Education, Recreation, and Dance* (March 1988), pp. 39-40.

54. "May Bar Events for Women From Future Olympic Games," *New York Times* (August 7, 1928), p. 15.

55. R. Korsgarrd, "A History of the American Amateur Union of the United States,"(Ed. D. dissertation), Teacher's College, Columbia University, New York, New York, 1952.

56. American Olympic Committee, *Report of the American Olympic Committee, Games of the Xth Olympiad, Los Angeles, California, 1932* (New York: AOC, 1932), p. 126. See also Gerber, et. al., *The American Woman in Sport*, p. 153.

57. Tunis, "Women and the Sports Business," *Harper's Monthly* (July 1929), p. 213.

58. "Editorial: A Challenge for Tomorrow," *Ladies' Home Journal* (October 1932), p. 20; Mary Roberts Rinehart, "Editorial. The Chaotic Decade," *Ladies' Home Journal* (May 1930), pp. 35, 172.

59. Barton S. Curie, "Editorial: Powder-Puff Pets," *Ladies' Home Journal* (February 1924), p. 32.

60. Advertisements for Hind's Lotion, *Ladies' Home Journal* (January 1937), p. 68; (April 1937), p. 106. All advertisements below are from *Ladies' Home Journal*.

61. Advertisements for Fleischmann's Yeast, (April 1937), p. 127; (January 1938), p. 67.

62. Advertisements for Woodbury's Soap, (July 1936), p. 41; (November 1936), p. 45; (February 1937), p. 67; (April 1937), p. 79; (February 1939), p. 45; (March 1939), p. 50.

63. Advertisements for Lux Soap, (April 1937), p. 73; (September 1938), p. 35; (July 1938), p. 57: (September 1938), p. 35, p. 67; (June 1938), p. 92.

64. Advertisement for Jergens Lotion, (February 1938), p. 52. Advertisements for Double Mint Chewing Gum, (September 1939), p. 67; (June 1938), p. 92.

65. Advertisement for Arch-Preserver Shoes, (November 1940), p. 101.

66. Advertisement for Franco-American Spaghetti (March 1938), p. 53.

67. Advertisement for Coco-Malt Drink Mix, (October 1938), p. 51.

68. Advertisements for Mum Deodorant, (July 1938), p. 51; (June 1938), p. 55.

69. Advertisement for Mum Deodorant, (May 1938), p. 65.

70. Advertisement for Lux Laundry Soap, (July 1938), p. 64.

71. Advertisementfor Lux Laundry Soap, (March 1938), p. 115.

72. Advertisement for Chase and Sanborn Coffee, (February 1937), p. 45.

73. Advertisement for Chrysler Motors, (April 1937), p. 100.

74. Twin, *Out of the Bleachers*, p. xxvii.

Epilogue

As the years passed, the image of the sportswoman steadily deteriorated. Even the athletic look disappeared as fashion once again changed, this time reflecting the partial return of the voluptuous look. Girdles made a strong comeback, along with high-heeled shoes and underwired, padded bras.[1] The reigning beauty queens of the next era illustrated this change very dramatically. Unlike Lily Langtry, women such as Jane Russell or Marilyn Monroe did not endorse the athletic look.

Depression-era social and economic developments which had spelled the demise of the sportswoman only intensified in the 1940s. World War II and ensuing rationing worked to exaggerate the varying levels of deprivation. Also during the war years, record numbers of women (over half of them married) joined the work-force to meet the demand for laborers. Many critics believed that taking women out of the home would lead to the breakdown of the family. The rising divorce rate and concerns over juvenile delinquency were eyed with great foreboding. The long Depression and war years produced a great desire to return to normalcy. Women were encouraged to return home and were bombarded by advertising campaigns which incessantly announced that domesticity was the most rewarding goal in life and that the housewife was the nation's most important institution. During an age in which any untraditional behavior on the part of women drew criticism, the sportswoman could hardly return.[2] Instead, the changed social conditions combined with the return of the voluptuous look would usher in a symbolic replacement for the sportswoman: the cheerleader. She was, as was her counterpart the beauty queen, chosen on the basis of her physical appearance and did not engage in sports herself.[3]

For several decades after the collapse of the women's sports movement, virtually no change occurred in the status quo. Despite student apathy and even opposition, play days and severely restricted games continued within the ranks of physical education. Nowhere were these restrictions so obvious as in the case of basketball. To protect women from excessive running and jumping, the rules provided only for a half-court game. Under this format, teams consisted of three offensive players and three defensive players. Jumping was discouraged and to limit running, restrictions were placed on the number of steps a player could take before having to pass the ball. Furthermore, rules stipulated that players could not cross the half court line. This format continued in some high schools into the 1980s.

Concern over the negative effects of sports on women's health also continued for several decades after the 1930s. In the 1960s, for example, the American Medical Association still advised women to refrain from most sports for fear that their breasts and reproductive organs might be damaged.[4] Also remarkably persistent was the belief that competitive sports were unwomanly. Decades after Paul Gallico quipped that women looked beautiful only in a few sports, a majority of people continued to believe that most sports were unfeminine except for the traditional ones such as swimming, tennis, or golf. Serious competition, however, was still frowned upon for women in these or other sports. [5]

It is quite obvious that things have changed a great deal. Today, popular magazines are once again replete with the image of the sportswoman. Fashion lauds the slim, muscular look, and health clubs are packed with men and women trying to conform to this ideal. In addition, sponsors pour million of dollars into women's sports events. Early critics of sports for women such as Arabella Kenealy, Paul Gallico, or John Tunis would undoubtedly boggle at the sight of women competing in marathons or in such industry-sponsored events as the Bud Light Triathlon Series or the Virginia Slims Tennis Tournaments. The last thirty years have indeed brought great changes in women's sports. A careful analysis of those changes would be a rewarding task for the historian.

Any brief examination of the re-emergence of the sportswoman would have to explore two developments: the women rights movement and the growth of medical specialties. Unlike the nineteenth century women's sports movement which grew out of a concern for health, its mid-twentieth century counterpart grew out of the campaigns for women's equality during the 1960s and 1970s. The demands for equal rights, equal pay, and equal access had profound implications for women's sports. Often hailed as the great landmark, the 1972 legislation known popularly as Title IX helped pave the way for the re-creation of women's sports by requiring that colleges which received federal money offer women equal access to sports programs.[6]

Developments within the medical profession also fostered the cause of the sportswoman by decisively silencing those critics who had feared that intense competition jeopardized the health of young women. The numerous medical authorities cited in this work who opposed women's sports offered no solid quantitative proof for their arguments. As medical specialties such as cardiology, gynecology, or exercise physiology developed, earlier qualitative indictments lost sway. The old adage that lasting health was built in early life also faded away. Today, men and women of all ages can not escape the message preached to them by the medical profession that exercise improves health and increases life span.

In addition to being confronted with reams of medical data, the observer can see first hand that women can indeed compete successfully in an extensive array of sporting events without ruining their health or endangering the race. It would be priceless to know what many early critics of women's sports would say if they could see a woman such as Norway's Grete Waits finishing ahead of thousands of men in her many victories in the New York Marathon, or perhaps better still to see the various women track stars pose for the cameras with their children.

Although much has changed, the question of limits still pervades women's sports, and the relationship of athletics to femininity remains a cloudy issue. Questions such as how aggressive, or how muscular a woman athlete should be are still raised. In the 1980s, for example, tennis fans were split in loyalty between the baseline play of Chris Evert and the aggressive net play of the more muscular Martina Navratilova. Even a sport which might be considered on the leading edge in the evolution of women's sports has had to confront the question of limits. In the 1980s, champion women bodybuilders demonstrated more heavily muscled physiques. As the 1990s began, a movement away from excessive bulk was beginning.

As in the past, so too in the future, changing fashions, styles, and tastes may decide the cultural limits of the sportswoman. By comparison, the sportswoman of the current day flourishes within a much sturdier institutional foundation than her 1920s counterpart. The great weakness of early women's sports was the lack of real sports stars. Today's sportswoman is not a hollow image created by fashion and advertising. The last thirty years have produced outstanding women athletes in an amazing diversity of fields, ranging from track and field to automobile racing. In addition, fitness has become such a vital and unquestioned part of medical advice that it is not likely to go out of style.

Changing fashions and tastes may yet decide the future of women's sports, but no collapse seems imminent, although economics may continue to play a crucial role. For both men's and women's sports at the elite level, high visibility sporting events are built on the bubble of television coverage and consequently upon the willingness of networks, sponsors, and advertisers to invest millions of dollars in those broadcasts. Loss of this revenue and coverage could in fact lead to a detrimental loss of visibility.

Epilogue Notes

1. Lois Banner, *American Beauty* (New York: Knoph, 1983), p. 285. See also, Claudia Glenn Dowling, "Ooh-La-La! The Bra," *Life* (June 1989), p. 92.

2. See among others, James Gilbert, *Another Chance: Postwar America, 1945-1968* Philadelphia: Temple University Press, 1981); William Chafe, *The American Woman. Her Changing Social, Economic, and Political Roles, 1920-1970* (New York: Oxford University Press, 1972); and Carl Degler, *At Odds, Women and the Family in America From the Revolution to the Present* (New York: Oxford University Press, 1980).

3. Banner, *American Beauty*, p. 293.

4. Cited in Rose and Hal Higdon, "What Sports for Girls?" *Today's Health* (October 1967), p. 21.

5. Paul Gallico, "Women in Sports Should Look Beautiful," *Reader's Digest* (August 1936), pp. 12-14; Stephanie Twin, *Out of the Bleachers: Writings on Women and Sport* (Old Westbury, N.Y.: Feminist Press, 1979), p. xxv.

6. Recent court decisions have interpreted Title IX more narrowly.

Bibliography

Primary Sources: Articles

"The Alleged Decline of Marriage." *Living Age* (July 8, 1899): 198-200.

Allen, Grant. "Plain Words on the Woman Question." *Popular Science* (December 1889): 170-181.

Arnold, E. H. "Athletics for Women." *American Physical Education Review* (October 1924): 452-457.

"Artificial Disabilities." *Woman's Journal* (January 4, 1873): 2.

"Athletic Strenuosity." *Journal of the American Medical Association* (July 1925): 270.

Baker, Arlo. "The Negative Side of Modern Athletics." *Forum* (May (1901)): 287-297.

Baldwin, Catherine. "Note on the Health of Women Students." *Century* (June 1891): 294-295.

Ballantine, Harriet. "Out-of-Door Sports for College Women." *American Physical Education Review* (March 1898): 38-43.

Barney, Elizabeth. "The American Sportswoman." *Fortnightly Review* (August 1894): 263-277.

Beckwith, Carrol. "Bouguereau." *Cosmopolitan* (January 1890): 259-264.

Benjamin, Louise Paine. "Sing or Swim." *Ladies' Home Journal* (July 1936): 24-25.

Bentley, Dr. Lillian. "Dr. Bentley's Physical Culture for Girls." *Ladies' Home Journal* (November 1909): 27.

"Bicycling Around New York." *Collier's* (April 27, 1901)

"Brain Work." *Godey's Ladies' Book* (November 1871): 473.

Britan, Nellie Hattan. "Physical Education, What it is Doing for Women." *Education* 29 (1908): 35-45.

Brooks, Lillian. "Golf for Women." *Collier's* (April 1, 1899): 11-12.

Burdick, W. "Safeguarding the Athletic Competition of Girls and Women." *American Physical Education Review* (May 1927): 367.

Carrington, Hereward. "Proper Food for Perfect Health." *Cosmopolitan* (August 1910): 326-330.

"Co-Education of the Sexes." *Woman's Journal* (January 4, 1873): 4.

"Concerning Disinfectants." *Nation* (June 1, 1866): 698.

"Concerning Disinfectants." *Nation* (June 5, 1866): 713-714.

Cooks, Dorothy. "Take Your Beauty Outdoors." *Ladies' Home Journal* (July 1934): 41.

Coops, Helen. "Sports for Women." *American Physical Education Review* (November 1926): 1086-1089.

"Country Life and its Advantages." *Godey's Ladies' Book* (October 1860): 366-367.

Cummings, Sidney. "Lawn Tennis as a Health Builder." in William F. Fleming. ed. *Physical Culture Classics* vol. 4. New York: E.B. Dumont, 1909.

Currie, Barton. "Editorial: Powder-Puff Pets." *Ladies' Home Journal* (February 1924): 32.

"Death In-Doors." *Godey's Ladies' Book* (November 1867): 449.

De Koven, Anna. "The Athletic Women." *Good Housekeeping* (August 1912): 148-157.

De Koven, Mrs. Reginald. "Bicycling for Women." *Cosmopolitan* (August 1895): 286-294.

Dix, Dorothy. "The Girls of To-day." *Good Housekeeping* (March 1916): 288-291.

"Do Americans Eat too Much?" *Collier's* (November 21, 1903): 1.

Dublin, Louis. "Longevity of College Athletes." *Harper's Monthly* (July 1928): 229-238.

E. B. S. "Kitchen Gymnastics." *Good Housekeeping* (January 1907): 118-119.

"Early Rising and Exercise." *Godey's Ladies' Book* (October 1864): 321-322.

"Editorial: A Challenge for Tomorrow." *Ladies' Home Journal* (October 1932): 20.

"Editorial: The Side that's Next to the Sun." *Ladies' Home Journal* (May 1898): 2.

"Editor's Study." *Forum* (November 1893): 961-962.

"Editors' Table: Health of American Women Deteriorating." *Godey's Ladies' Book* (November 1870): 471.

"Editors' Table: The Physical Training of Girls." *Godey's Ladies' Book* (November 1870): 471.

"Editors' Table: Vassar College Opened." *Godey's Ladies' Book* (August 1865): 173.

"Editors' Table: Weariness of the World and its Work." *Godey's Ladies' Book* (August 1864): 173.

"The Education of Girls." *Nation* (September 26, 1878): 184-195.

"The Education of Women." *Nation* (August 30, 1866): 165-166.

Eliot, Charles. "The Normal American Woman." *Ladies' Home Journal* (January 1908): 15.

"Exercise for Girls." *Godey's Ladies' Book* (July 1867): 80-81.

"Extracts, Abstracts and Notices of Magazine Articles." *American Physical Education Review* (July 1925): 523-524.

"Facts and Opinions About the Cholera." *Nation* (April 26, 1866): 520-521.

Fallows, Alice. "Basket Ball: A Builder up of Vigorous Women." *Good Housekeeping* (March 1902): 197-201.

"A Few Words About Cholera." *Nation* (September 7, 1865): 306-308.

Finck, Henry. "Are Womanly Women Doomed?" *Independent* (January 1901): 267-271.

Francis, Henry Waldorf. "Marriage and Dress." *Arena* (March 1902): 292-296.

"Free Muscular Development." *Harper's* (May 1878): 915-924.

Garrigues, Henry. "Woman and the Bicycle." *Forum* (January 1896): 578-587.

Greely-Smith, Nixola. "New York Women and the Art of Fencing." *Illustrated Sporting News* (January 9, 1904): 4-5.

Gregory, Dr. Samuel. "Female Physicians." *Living Age* (May 3, 1862): 243.

Gulick, Dr. Luther Halsey. "Athletics Do Not Test Womanliness." *American Physical Education Review* (September 1906): 157-160.

"Gymnastics." *Atlantic Monthly* (March 1861): 283-302.

"Gymnastics." *North American Review* (July 1855): 51-69.

Habberton, John. "Open Air Recreation for Women." *Outing* (November 1885): 160-161.

Harris, Dr. Elisha. "Cholera Prevention." *Nation* (October 3, 1867): 273.

Harrison, Mrs. Burton. "Henley Week." *Cosmopolitan* (July 1900): 241-252.

"The Health and Physical Habits of English and American Women." *Scribner's Monthly* (April 1874): 747-754.

"Health in Great Cities." *Nation* (May 11, 1866): 600-601.

"The Health of American Women." *Nation* (October 8, 1885): 295-296.

"The Health of American Women." *North American Review* (December 1882): 503-504.

"The Health of Our Girls." *Atlantic Monthly* (June 1862): 722-731.

"Health Statistics for Women." *Woman's Journal* (October 17, 1885): 330.

Herrick, Christine Terhune. "Schoolgirl Athletes in Track and Field." *Illustrated Sporting News* (June 1903): 14-15.

Hill, Lucille. "The New Athletics." *Wellesley College News* (October 29, 1902): 1.

"Hints About Health." *Godey's Ladies' Book* (September 1867): 265.

"Housework as an Aid to Health Culture." *Good Housekeeping* (December 1901): 292-295.

Hough, Charles M.D. "How to Avoid Taking Cold." *Cosmopolitan* (October 1893): 683-685.

Hutchinson, Woods M.D. "The Bugbear of Exercise." *Good Housekeeping* (December 1913): 817-823.

_____. "Fat and its Follies." *Cosmopolitan* (February 1910): 383-389.

_____. "The Secret of Beauty." *Good Housekeeping* (March 1916): 326-327.

Hyde, William DeWitt. "A Rational System of Physical Training." *Forum* (June 1891): 446-452.

"Is Athletic Training Overdone." *Illustrated Sporting News* (March 1904): 1.

Jackson, Kate. "How Shall Women Dress?" *North American Review* (June 1885): 568-571.

Kellor, Francis. "Ethical Value of Sports for Women." *American Physical Education Review* (September 1906): 160-171.

Kenealy, Arabella. "Woman as an Athlete." *Living Age* (April 29, 1899): 363-370.

_____. "Woman as an Athlete. A Rejoinder." *Living Age* (July 22, 1899): 201-213.

Lapham, Ella. "Woman's Duty to Woman." *Forum* (July 1886): 455-467.

Laurvik, J. Nilsen. "The American Girl Out-of-Doors." *Woman's Home Companion* (August 1912): 17.

Lee, Mabel. "The Case For and Against Intercollegiate Athletics for Women and the Situation as it Stands Today." *American Physical Education Review* (January 1924): 13-19.

_____. "The Case For and Against Intercollegiate Athletics for Women and the Situation Since 1923." *Research Quarterly* (May 1931): 93-127.

_____. "A Consideration of the Fundamental Differences Between Boys and Girls as They Affect the Girls' Programs of Physical Education." *Education* (April 1933): 468.

Linton, E. Lynn. "The Higher Education of Women." *Fortnightly Review* 464 (1886): 498-510.

_____. "The Revolt Against Matrimony." *Forum* (January 1891): 585-595.

Loomis, Charles. "The California Girl." *Good Housekeeping* (October 1903): 287-290.

Lyon, Paulina Harriette. "The Only Woman's Athletic Club." *Collier's* (August 24, 1901):

H.M. "Growing Young Again." *Good Housekeeping* (February 1906): 231.

McCurdy, Persis Harlow. "The History of Physical Training at Mount Holyoke College." *American Physical Education Review* (March 1909): 138-150.

Macfadden, Bernarr. "Building Vitality." in William F. Fleming, ed. *Physical Culture Classics* vol. 2 (New York: E.B. Dumont 1909).

_____. "The Development of Grace, Suppleness and Symmetry." in William F. Fleming, ed. *Physical Culture Classics* vol. 4 (New York : E. B. Dumont 1909).

_____. "Health Made and Preserved by Daily Exercise." *Cosmopolitan* (April 1903): 705-712.

MacFarlane, Peter Clark. "Schools of Fun and Fellowship." *Good Housekeeping* (May 1914): 84-593.

Mahé, Edouard. "Beauties of the French Stage." *Cosmopolitan* (March 1891): 513-528.

"May Bar Events for Women From Future Olympic Games." *New York Times* (August 7, 1928): 15.

Meltzer, Charles Henry. "Franz Von Stuck, Painter and Pagan." *Cosmopolitan* (June 1912): 83-90.

_____. "Frederick MacMonnies, Sculptor." *Cosmopolitan* (July 1912): 207-211.

"Miss Cartwright Wins Three Titles." *New York Times* (July 5, 1928): 15.

"Modish Raiment for the Sportswoman." *Illustrated Sporting News* (May 7, 1904): 16.

Moffett, Cleveland. "Luxurious Newport." *Cosmopolitan* (August 1907): 349-358.

Mullett, Mary. "A Swarm of Twelve Hundred Girls." *Ladies' Home Journal* (June 1906): 5-6.

Murray, Grace Peckham. "The Peril of Obesity." *Collier's* (June 29, 1901): 17.

Nash, Jay. "Athletics for Girls." *North American Review* (January 1928): 100.

"The New Gymnastics." *Atlantic Monthly* (August 1862): 129-148.

"Notes on Cholera." *Nation* (October 5, 1871): 229-230.

O'Dell, Maude. "Building a Physical Culture Girl." in William F. Fleming, ed. *Physical Culture Classics* vol. 4 (New York: E.B. Dumont 1909).

O'Hagan, Anne. "The Athletic Girl." *Munsey's Magazine* (August 1901): 729-738.

Oswald, F. L. "The Age of Gymnastics." *Popular Science* June 1878): 129-139.

"The Other Side of the Question." *Nation* (October 17, 1867): 316-317.

Ottendorfer, Oswald. "Are Our Immigrants to Blame?" *Forum* (July 1891): 541-549.

"Outstanding Problems of Girls' Athletics." *American Physical Education Review* (May 1926): 846-848.

Paine, Elizabeth. "Athletics at Women's Colleges, Smith, Mount Holyoke, Bryn Mawr." *Illustrated Sporting News* (July 9, 1904): 3-6.

Patterson, Ethel Lloyd. "Why Grow Old?" *Ladies' Home Journal* (July 1922): 7.

Peck, Harry Thurston. "The Woman of Fascination." *Cosmopolitan* (November 1898): 71-83.

Penny, Virginia. "Poor Health of American Women." *Ladies' Repository* (March 1865): 155-157.

Porter, Charlotte. "Physical Hindrances to Teaching Girls." *Forum* (September 1891): 41-49.

The Principal of One of the Largest Girls' High Schools in America. "The Girl at the Head of Her Class." *Ladies' Home Journal* (January 1912): 24.

Putnam, Granville. "The Introduction of Gymnastics in New England." *New England Magazine* (September 1890): 110-113.

Pyke, Radford. "Strength in Women's Features." *Cosmopolitan* (November 1904): 111-114.

Richardson, Sophia Foster. "Tendencies in Athletics for Women in Colleges and Universities." *Popular Science* (February 1897): 517-522.

Rickert, Edith. "Has the College Injured the Health of Girls?" *Ladies' Home Journal* (January 1912): 11-12.

Rinehart, Mary Roberts. "Editorial: The Chaotic Decade." *Ladies' Home Journal* (May 1930): 35, 172.

Roosevelt, Theodore. "The Law of Civilization and Decay." *Forum* (January 1897): 575-589.

Saleeby, C.W. "The Purpose of Womanhood." *Forum* (January 1911): 44-50.

Sandys, Edwyn. "The Place that Women Occupy in Sport." *Illustrated Sporting News* (November 21, 1903): 1.

Sangster, Margaret. "From a Woman's Viewpoint." *Collier's* (June 16, 1900): 17.

_____. "From a Woman's Viewpoint." *Collier's* (June 30, 1900): 17.

_____. "From a Woman's Viewpoint." *Collier's* (April 13, 1901): 16.

_____. "Girls Problems." *Ladies' Home Journal* (April 1902): 2.

"Sanitary Drainage." *Nation* (July 6, 1876): 13-14.

Sargent, Dudley. "After a Woman is Forty." *Ladies' Home Journal* (April 1912): 13.

_____. "Are Athletics Making Girls Masculine?" *Ladies' Home Journal* (March 1912): 11, 71-73.

_____. "The Gymnasium of a Great University." *Cosmopolitan* (May 1890): 40-50.

_____. "How Can I Have a Graceful Figure?" *Ladies' Home Journal* (February 1912): 15-16.

_____. "The Physical Development of Women." *Scribner's Magazine* (February 1889): 172-185.

_____. "What Athletic Games are Injurious to Women?" *American Physical Education Review* (September 1906): 174-181.

Schuyler, Montgomery. "A Newport Palace." *Cosmopolitan* (August 1900): 361-371.

Sears, Anna Wentworth. "The Modern Women Out-of-Doors." *Cosmopolitan* (september 1896): 630-640.

Sinclair, Upton. "Starving for Health's Sake." *Cosmopolitan* (May 1910): 739-746.

"Slaughter-Houses and Health." *Nation* (October 4, 1866): 273-274.

Smith, A. Lapthorn, M.D. "Higher Education of Women and Race Suicide." *Popular Science* (March 1905): 466-473.

"The Sportswoman." *Illustrated Sporting News* (February 6, 1904): 16.

"A Star of the North." *Cosmopolitan* (March 1913): 552-553.

Starrett, Helen Ekin. "The Future of Our Daughters." *Forum* (October 1890): 185-196.

Tabor, Francis. "Directed Sport as a Factor in Education." *Forum* (May 1899): 320-324.

Taylor, Frank. "Fast and Pretty." *Collier's* (August 20, 1938).

"The Thoughtful Hour." *Good Housekeeping* (August 1899): 92-93.

Thwing, Charles. "Women's Education." *Education* (1883): 53-62.

Tunis, John R. "The Olympic Games." *Harper's Monthly* (August 1928): 314-323.

_____. "Women and the Sport Business." *Harper's Monthly* (July 1929): 211-221.

"Two Girls." *Nation* (February 6, 1868): 107-109.

Uhle, Dr. Charles P. "Face Powders and Paints." *Godey's Ladies' Book* (February 1869): 189.

_____. "Health Department." *Godey's Ladies' Book* (February 1871): 191-192.

_____. "Health Department." *Godey's Ladies' Book* (April 1871): 381-382.

_____. "Health Department." *Godey's Ladies' Book* (March 1873): 184.

_____. "Health Department." *Godey's Ladies' Book* (April 1873): 376.

"United States Captures Two Olympic Events." *New York Times* (August 1, 1928): 1, 16.

"Vassar College." *Nation* (May 19, 1870): 315-317.

"Vitality Versus Disease." *Living Age* (April 5, 1862): 27.

Waddle, Eleanor. "Side Glances at American Beauty." *Cosmopolitan* (June 1890): 193-202.

Walker, Emma, M.D. "Good Health for Girls." *Ladies' Home Journal* (March 1902): 33.

_____. "Good Health for Girls." *Ladies' Home Journal* (April 1902): 33.

_____. "Good Health for Girls." *Ladies' Home Journal* (June 1902): 31.

_____. "Pretty Girl Questions." *Ladies' Home Journal* (October 1908): 54.

Wayman, Agnes. "Women's Athletics: All Uses, No Abuses." *American Physical Education Review* (November 1924): 517-519.

"Weak Lungs and How to Make Them Strong." *Atlantic Monthly* (June 1863): 657-674.

"Wet Nurses." *Godey's Ladies' Book* (July 1860): 81.

"When a Girl is at College." *Ladies' Home Journal* (September 1909): 32.

Willard, Frances. "How I Learned to Ride the Bicycle." in Stephanie Twin. ed. *Out of the Bleachers. Writings on Women and Sport* (Old Westbury, New York: Feminist Press, 1979): 103-114.

Williams, Wythe. "Americans Beaten in Four Olympic Tests." *New York Times* (August 3, 1928): 3.

Wilson, Dr. Jonathan Stainback. "Health Department." *Godey's Ladies' Book* (March 1860): 275-276.

_____. "Health Department." *Godey's Ladies' Book* (September 1863): 277-278.

_____. "How Girls Should be Clothed." *Godey's Ladies' Book* (March 1863): 307.

Wilson, Mrs. Woodrow. "The Woman of Fifty." *Cosmopolitan* (March 1903): 503-512.

Winchester, Boyd. "The New Woman." *Arena* (April 1902): 367-373.

Wingate, Charles. "Some Famous Hermonies of the Past." *Cosmopolitan* (January 1890): 314-323.

Youmans, Edward. "The Higher Education of Women." *Popular Science* (April 1874): 748-750.

Young, C. A. "College Athletic Sports." *Forum* (October 1886): 142-152.

"A Young Man's Fancy." *Good Housekeeping* (April 1910): 424-425.

Primary Sources: Books

Adam, G. Mercer. *Sandow on Physical Training. A Study in Perfect Form.* New York: Selwin Tait and Sons, 1894.

Adams, Brook. *Law of Civilization and Decay.* New York: MacMillan, 1886. Reprinted by Vintage Press, 1955.

Alcott, William. *Physiology of Marriage.* Boston, 1866.

_____. *The Young Woman's Book of Health.* Boston: Tappan, Whittemore and Mason, 1850.

American Olympic Committee. *Report of the American Olympic Committee. Ninth Olympic Games, Amsterdam, 1928.* New York: A.O.C. Publications, 1928.

_____. *Report of the American Olympic Committee. Games of the Xth Olympiad, Los Angeles, California, 1932.* New York: A.O.C. Publications, 1932.

Beard, George. *American Nervousness. Its Causes and Consequences.* New York: Putnam's Sons, 1881. Reprinted by Arno Press, 1972.

Beecher, Catherine. *Physiology and Calisthenics for Schools and Families.* New York, 1856.

Blaikie, William. *How to Get Strong and How to Stay So.* New York: Harper and Brothers, 1879.

Castle, William. et. al. *Heredity and Eugenics.* Chicago: University of Chicago Press, 1912.

Claghorn, Kate Holladay. *College Training for Women.* New York: Thomas Crowell, 1897.

Clarke, Edward H. *Sex in Education; or a Fair Chance for the Girls.* Boston: Rand, Avery and Co., 1873. Reprinted ed. Arno Press, 1972.

Dixon, Edward H. *Woman and Her Diseases. From the Cradle to the Grave: Adapted Exclusively to Her Instruction in the Physiology of Her System, and All the Diseases of Her Critical Periods.* 10th ed. Philadelphia: G.G. Evans, 1860.

Dowd, Daniel. *Physical Culture. For Home and School, Scientific and Practical.* New York: Fowler-Wells, 1888.

Fleming, William F., ed. *Physical Culture Classics.* 4 vols. New York: E. B. Dumont, 1909.

Frymir, Alice. *Track and Field for Women.* New York: Barnes, 1930.

Gallico, Paul. *Farewell to Sports.* New York: Knopf, 1938.

Gardiner, Augustus Kinsley. *Conjugal Sins Against the Laws of Life and Health.* New York: Redfield, 1870. Reprinted by Arno Press, 1974.

Grant, Madison. *The Passing of the Great Race. The Racial Basis of European History.* New York: Scribner's Son's, 1916.

Hall, Prescott. *Immigration and its Effects Upon the United States.* New York: Holt and Co., 1906.

Howe, Julia Ward. *Sex and Education. A Reply to Dr. E. H. Clarke's "Sex in Education".* Boston: Roberts Brothers, 1874. Reprinted by Arno Press, 1972.

Kellerman, Annette. *Physical Beauty. How to Keep Fit.* New York: Geo. Duran, 1918.

Lewis, Dio. *Our Girls.* New York: Harper and Brother, 1871.

_____. *The New Gymnastics for Men, Women, and Children.* Boston: Tichenor and Fields, 1862.

Macfadden, Bernarr. *Muscular Power and Beauty. Containing Detailed Instruction for the Development of the External Muscular System to its Utmost Degree of Perfection.* New York: Physical Culture Publishing, 1906.

Mitchell, S. Weir. *Fat and Blood*. Philadelphia: Lippincott, 1887.

Noel, E. B., and Clark, J. O. M. *A History of Tennis*. Vol. 1, London: Oxford, 1924.

Ross, Edward A. *The Old World in the New. The Significance of Past and Present Immigration to the American People*. New York: Century, 1914.

Savage, Howard J., et. al. *Current Development in American Sport*. New York: Carnegie Foundation for the Advancement of Teaching, Bulletin 26, 1931.

Strong, Josiah. *The Challenge of the City*. New York: The Young People's Missionary Movement, 1907.

_____. *The New Era, or the Coming Kingdom*. New York: Baker and Taylor, 1893.

_____. *Our Country. Its Possible Future and its Present Crisis*. rev. ed. New York: Baker and Taylor, 1891.

Treloar, Albert. *Treloar's Science of Muscular Development; A Textbook of Physical Training*. New York: Physical Culture Publishing Co., 1904.

Woolson, Abba Gould, ed. *Dress Reform: A Series of Lectures Delivered in Boston on Dress as it Affects the Health of Women*. Boston: Roberts Brothers, 1874. reprint ed. Arno Press, 1974.

Secondary Sources: Articles

Allen, Francis Robbins. "Public Health Work in the Southeast, 1872-1941: The Study of a Social Movement." Ph.D. dissertation. University of North Carolina, 1946.

Blake, John B. "The Inoculation Controversy in Boston, 1721-1722." in Judith Walzer Leavitt and Ronald L. Numbers, *eds. Sickness and Health in America* 2d. ed. Madison: University of Wisconsin Press, 1985.

Bullough, Vera. "Merchandising the Sanitary Napkin: Lillian Gilbreth's 1927 Survey." *Signs* (Spring 1985): 615-627.

Davenport, JoAnna. "The Role of Women in the International Olympic Committee." *Journal of Physical Education Recreation and Dance.* (March 1988): 42.

Dewing, Roland. "History of American Sports: Academic Featherbedding or Neglected Area?" *Social Science Journal* (October 1977).

Duffy, John. "Social Impact of Disease in the Late Nineteenth Century." in Judith Walzer Leavitt and Ronald L. Numbers eds. *Sickness and Health in America* 2d. ed. Madison: University of Wisconsin Press. 1985.

George, Judith Jenkins. "Mary Washburn Conklin. Pioneer in Women's Olympic Track and Field." *Journal of Physical Education, Recreation and Dance* (March 1988): 37-41.

Gerber, Ellen. "The Controlled Development of Collegiate Sport for Women." *Journal of Sport History* (Spring 1975).

Golden, Janet. "From Wet-Nurse Directory to Milk Bank: The Delivery of Human Milk in Boston." *Bulletin of the History of Medicine* (Winter 1988): 589-605.

Guttmann, Allen. "Commentary: Who's on First? Or, Books on the History of American Sports." *Journal of American History* (September 1979): 348-354.

Hamlin, Christopher. "Providence and Putrefaction: Victorian Sanitarians and the Natural Theology of Health and Disease." in Patrick Brantinger, ed. *Energy and Entrophy. Science and Culture in Victorian Britain.* Bloomington: Indiana University Press. 1989.

Hudson, Robert P. "The Biography of Disease; Lessons from Chlorosis." *Bulletin of the History of Medicine* Summer 1977): 448-463.

Korsgaard, Robert. "A History of the American Athletic Union of the United States." Ed. D. Dissertation. Teacher's College, Columbia University, New York, New York. 1952.

Leigh, Mary. "The Evolution of Women's Participation in the Summer Olympic Games, 1900-1948." Ph.D. Dissertation. Ohio State University, Columbus, Ohio. 1974.

Morantz, Regina Markel. "Making Women Modern; Middle Class Women and Health Reform in Nineteenth Century America." *Journal of Social History* (June 1977): 490-501.

Owens, Larry. "Pure and Sound Government. Laboratories, Playing Fields, and Gymnasia in the Nineteenth-Century Search for Order." *Isis* (June 1985): 182-194.

Pernick, Martin S. "Politics, Parties, and Pestilence: Epidemic Yellow Fever in Philadelphia and the Rise of the First Party System." in Judith Walzer Leavitt and Ronald L. Numbers. eds. *Sickness and Health in America.* 2d. ed. Madison: University of Wisconsin Press. 1985.

Rosenberg, Charles E. "The Therapeutic Revolution: Medicine, Meaning, and Social Change in Nineteenth-Century America." in Judith Walzer Leavitt and Ronald L. Numbers. eds. *Sickness and Health in America.* Madison: University of Wisconsin Press. 1985.

Sicherman, Barbara. "The Uses of a Diagnosis: Doctors, Patients, and Neurasthenia." in Judith Walzer Leavitt and Ronald L. Numbers. eds. *Sickness and Health in America.* Madison: University of Wisconsin Press. 1985.

Smith-Rosenberg, Carroll. "The Female Animal: Medical and Biological Views of Women." in Charles Rosenberg, *No Other Gods. On Science and American Social Thought.* Baltimore: The Johns-Hopkins University Press. 1961.

_____. "Puberty to Menopause; The Cycle of Femininity in Nineteenth-Century America." in Mary Hartman and Lois Banner. eds. *Clio's Conscience Raised. New Perspectives on the History of Women.* New York: Harper Colophon. 1974.

Spears, Betty. "The Emergence of Women in Sport." in Barbara J. Hoepner. ed. *Women's Athletics: Coping with Controversy.* Washington, D.C.: AAHPER Publications. 1974.

Trecker, Janice Law. "Sex, Science and Education." *American Quarterly* (October 1974): 352-366.

Waller-Zuckerman, Mary Ellen. "'Old Homes in a City of Perpetual Change': Women's Magazines, 1890-1920." *Business History Review* Winter, 1989: 715-714.

Whorton, James. "Patient Heal Thyself: Popular Health Reform Movements as Unorthodox Medicine." in Norman Gevitz. ed. *Other Healers. Unorthodox Medicine in America.* Baltimore: John Hopkins University Press. 1988.

Wood, Ann Douglass. "'The Fashionable Diseases': Women's Complaints and their Treatment in Nineteenth-Century America." *Journal of Interdisciplinary History* (Summer 1973).

Secondary Sources: Books

Ainsworth, Dorothy S. *The History of Physical Education in Colleges for Women. As Illustrated by Barnard, Bryn Mawr, Elmira, Goucher, Mills, Mount Holyoke, Radcliffe, Rockford, Smith, Vassar, Wellesley, and Wells.* New York: A S. Barnes, 1930.

Allen, Frederick Lewis. *Only Yesterday; An Informal History of the Nineteen-Twenties.* New York: Harper, 1931.

Banner, Lois. *American Beauty.* New York: Knopf, 1983.

Barrett, Richmond. *Good Old Summer Days. Newport, Narragansett Pier, Saratoga, Long Beach, Bar Harbor.* Boston: Houghton-Mifflin, 1952.

Berg, Barbara. *The Remembered Gate. Origins of American Feminism: The Woman and the City, 1800-1860.* New York: Oxford University Press, 1980.

Bledstein, Burton J. *The Culture of Professionalism. The Middle-Class and the Development of Higher Education in America.* New York: Norton, 1976.

Brantinger, Patrick, ed. *Energy and Enthropy. Science and Culture in Victorian Britain*. Bloomington: Indiana University Press, 1989.

Cassedy, James. *Medicine and American Growth, 1800-1860*. Madison: University of Wisconsin Press, 1986.

Chafe, William. *The American Woman. Her Changing Social, Economic, and Political Roles, 1920-1970*. New York: Oxford University Press, 1972.

Chambers, J. S. *The Conquest of Cholera. America's Greatest Scourge*. New York: Macmillan, 1938.

Cogan, Frances. *All-American Girl The Ideal of Real Womanhood in Mid-Nineteenth-Century America*. Athens: University of Georgia Press, 1989.

Cravens, Hamilton. *The Triumph of Evolution. American Scientists and the Heredity-Environment Controversy, 1900-1941*. Philadelphia: University of Pennsylvania, 1978.

Dana, Nathalie. *Young in New York: A Memoir of a Victorian Girlhood*. Garden City, N.J.: Doubleday, 1962.

Degler, Carl. *At Odds. Women and the Family in America from the Revolution to the Present*. New York: Oxford University Press, 1980.

Delamont, Sara and Duffin, Lorna. *The Nineteenth-Century Woman. Her Cultural And Physical World*. New York: Barnes and Noble, 1978.

Dijkstra, Bram. *Idols of Perversity. Fantasies of a Feminine Evil in Fin-de-Siecle Culture*. New York: Oxford University Press, 1986.

Edwards, Harry. *The Revolt of the Black Athlete*. New York: Free Press, 1969.

Ehrenreich, Barbara, and English, Deidre. *For Her Own Good: One Hundred Fifty Years of the Experts' Advice to Women*. Garden City, New York: Anchor, 1978.

Forster, Margaret. *Significant Sisters. The Grassroots of Active Feminism, 1839-1939*. New York: Oxford University Press, 1986.

152

Frankfort, Roberta. *College Women: Domesticity and Career in Turn of the Century America.* New York: New York University Press, 1977.

Friedan, Betty. *The Feminine Mystique.* New York: Norton, 1963.

Gerber, Ellen, et. al. *The American Woman in Sport.* Reading, Ma.: Addison-Wesley, 1974.

Gevitz, Norman, ed. *Other Healers. Unorthodox Medicine in America.* Baltimore: Johns-Hopkins University Press, 1988.

Green, Harvey. *Fit for America. Health, Fitness, Sport, and American Society.* New York: Pantheon, 1986.

_____. *The Light of the Home. An Intimate View of the Lives of Women in Victorian America.* New York: Pantheon, 1983.

Haller, Mark M. *Eugenics, Hereditarian Attitudes in American Thought.* New Brunswick: Rutgers University Press, 1963.

Hartman, Mary and Banner, Lois, eds. *Clio's Conscience Raised. New Perspectives on the History of Women.* New York: Harper Colophon, 1974.

Higham, John. *Strangers in the Land. Patterns of American Nativism.* rev. ed. New York: Atheneum, 1971.

Hoch, Paul. *Rip Off the Big Game. The Exploitation of Sports by the Power Elite.* Garden City, N.Y.: Anchor Books, 1972.

Hoepner, Barbara J., ed. *Women's Athletics: Coping with Controversy.* Washington, D.C.: AAHPER Publications, 1974.

Horowitz, Helen Lefkowitz. *Alma Mater: Design and Experience in Women's Colleges from their Nineteenth Century Beginnings to the 1930s.* New York: Knopf, 1984.

Howell, Reet, ed. *Her Story in Sport.* New York: Leisure Press, 1982.

Hugman, Barry. *The Olympic Games. Complete Track and Field Results, 1896-1988.* New York: Facts on File, 1988.

Leavitt, Judith Walzer. *Brought to Bed. Child Bearing in America, 1750-1950.* New York: Oxford University Press, 1986.

Leavitt, Judith Walzer and Numbers, Ronald L., eds. *Sickness and Health in America. Readings in the History of Medicine and Public Health.* 2d. ed. Madison: University of Wisconsin Press, 1985.

Levenstein, Harvey. *Revolution at the Table. The Transformation of the American Diet.* New York: Oxford University Press, 1988.

Ludmerer, Kenneth. *Genetics and American Society. A Historical Appraisal.* Baltimore: Johns-Hopkins University Press, 1972.

Marchand, Roland. *Advertising the American Dream. Making Way for Modernity.* Berkeley: University of California Press, 1985.

Matthews, Glenna. *"Just a Housewife": The Rise and Fall of Domesticity in America.* New York: Oxford University Press, 1987.

Morantz-Sanchez, Reginia Markel. *Sympathy and Science. Women's Physicians in American Medicine.* New York: Oxford University Press, 1985.

Mrozek, David. *Sport and American Mentality, 1880-1910.* Knoxville: University of Tennessee Press, 1983.

Newman, Louise Michelle, ed. *Men's Ideas/Women's Realities. Popular Science, 1870-1915.* New York: Pergamon Press, 1985.

Oppenheim, Janet, *"Shattered Nerves." Doctors, Patients, and Depression in Victorian England.* New York: Oxford University Press, 1991.

Parker, Gail, ed. *The Oven Birds. American Women on Womanhood, 1820-1920.* Garden City, New York: Anchor Books, 1972.

Riess, Steven. *The American Sporting Experience.* New York: Leisure Press, 1984.

_____. *Touching Base. Professional Baseball and American Culture in the Progressive Era.* Westport, Conn.: Greenwood Press, 1980.

Risse, Guenter B., et. al. *Medicine Without Doctors. Home Health Care in American History.* New York: Science History Publications, 1977.

Rosenberg, Charles. *The Care of Strangers. The Rise of the Hospital System.* New York: Basic Books, 1987.

_____. *The Cholera Years. The United States in 1832, 1849, 1866.* Chicago: University of Chicago Press, 1962.

_____. *No Other Gods. On Science and American Social Thought.* Baltimore: Johns-Hopkins University Press, 1961.

Shaw, Gary. *Meat on the Hoof. The Hidden World of Texas Football.* New York: St. Martin's Press, 1974.

Smelser, Marshall. *The Life that Ruth Built: A Biography.* New York: Quadrangle, 1975.

Smith-Rosenberg, Carroll. *Disorderly Conduct. Visions of Gender in Victorian America.* New York: Oxford University Press, 1986.

Solomon, Barbara M. *In the Company of Educated Women: A History of Women and Higher Education in America.* New Haven: Yale University Press, 1985.

Twin, Stephanie L., ed. *Out of the Bleachers: Writings on Women and Sport.* Old Westbury, N.Y.: The Feminist Press, 1979.

United States Lawn Tennis Association. *Fifty Years of Lawn Tennis in the United States.* New York: USLTA Publications, 1931.

Verbrugge, Martha H. *Able-Bodied Womenhood. Personal Health and Social Change in Nineteenth Century Boston.* New York: Oxford University Press, 1988.

Walters, Ronald. *American Reformers, 1815-1860.* New York: Hill and Wang, 1978.

Warner, John Harley. *The Therapeutic Perspective. Medical Practice, Knowledge, and Identity in America, 1820-1865.* Cambridge: Harvard University Press, 1986.

Wiebe, Robert. *The Search for Order, 1877-1920*. New York: Hill and Wang, 1967.

Whorton, James. *Crusaders for Fitness. The History of American Health Reformers*. Princeton: Princeton University Press, 1982.

Woody, Thomas. *A History of Education in the United States*. 2 vols. New York: Science Press, 1929.

Index